Walk with God!

Many Bles

Pastor

D0962129

Face Your Own Goliath!

Face Your Own **Goliath!**

Greg and Dianna

Moore

Recovery & Redemption Publishers
Denver, Colorado

Recovery & Redemption Publishers
P. O Box 461268
Aurora, Colorado 80015
Roar@recoveryandredemptionpub.com
$19.95 USD

Face Your Own Goliath! Is available at special quantity discounts for bulk
purchases. For special needs, books and book excerpts can be designed.

FYOG Recovery and Redemption Seminars available contact:
roar@recoveryandredemptionpub.com

Editor: N. Alston
Cover Art/Illustrations/Layout: JKat Designs   www.jkat-designs.com

"Roar!"™

The Face Your Own Goliath "Roar!" trademark is intended to remind each of us to find our own voice,

*our own courage, and our own purpose- **NOW!***

Dedication

This book is dedicated to our children and grandchildren. You are a blessing from God. It is the prayer of our hearts that this book be a blessing to each of you.

Greg's Acknowledgements

I would like to acknowledge and thank the following people for their contributions to our lives and ultimately, to this book:

Charles and Virginia Moore for seeing me through some very dark hours;

John Joslin, Ron Newman, John Winn, Jim Schneck, and Wes Sthole for their unending patience and wisdom as mentors;

Father Payo, Father Rick, Kenneth and Grady Jean Clark, Liz Picker, Jim Weber, Bob Litsheim, Charles Jones, Bishop Leonard and the Staff at Heritage Christian Center for their teaching and spiritual covering;

Dale Morris, Tom Kutch, Bob MacDonald, Bill Story, and Loren Couch for being Samuels in my life;

Devonee Grams, Sonny and Becky Wilson, for their faithful service and support;

All the members of the Celebrate Recovery Ministry at the Canyon View Vineyard Church in Grand Junction, CO;

The Leadership Team and members of Celebrate Recovery at Heritage Christian Center who courageously stepped forward to serve and confront their giants;

Tamara and Eddie Olson for their unflagging love, wisdom, support, and encouragement;

The Celebrate Recovery National Team for their faithful service in the field of recovery;

The countless brave individuals who have shared their experience, strength, and hope with us as they have Faced Their Own Goliaths;

The Pastors and staff of Crossroads Community Church Campus network;

My Family:

Justin Moore;

Chris, Stephanie, Carson, and Cole Mestas;

Nick, Melissa, Caden, Aubree, and Cruze Hanson;

Charlie Moore and Heather Hopper;

Darren, Chantielle, Braeden, and Kaelin Hanson;

Betsy and Brad Clapp, Cherry and Jim King, Stan and Kiki Moore, and Tom and Merry Brookes; all of whom have stood by me through good times and bad.

Cecelia Moore for two fine sons;

Paul Rosenberg and Nick Alston, whose belief in us and this project and whose indefatigable effort and support carried it to fruition, for his true heart of love for the Lord and service to others;

And:

Dianna Moore, my wife, Co-Author and best friend, whose love, insight, prayers, and challenges have been crucial to the ultimate form of the Book and the message it brings.

Thank you to each and every one of you.

I love you.

Greg Moore

Dianna's Acknowledgements

I would like to acknowledge and thank the following people for their contributions to my life and ultimately to this book:

God for deciding on my conception and choosing my parents;
My mother, Eloise Brownson Burdick Meyer, Jim Burdick for loving me by giving me a birth name and including me in his family and my real dad (who I do not know and who I hope to know soon) for conceiving me into this world;
My Grandmother Brownson for praying for me and instilling a spiritual life in me as I was growing up;
Teachers Judy Butterbaugh and Teri Hill for believing in me when I could not see it;
Curriculum at NITI, Calmar, IA;
Curriculum at Clarke College, Dubuque, IA;
Alcoholics Anonymous program;
Mary Catherine, Inga, Sharon, Sally, Louise, Dene-awesome sponsors through the years; and holding me accountable for my life, helping me stay sober, and gifting me with emotional sobriety!
Dubuque, IA Turning Point Treatment Center;
Karen and Karen for help processing through the death of my daughter;
Dubuque, IA AA meetings; Baraboo and Mazomaine WI AA Meetings
Granby, CO AA Club;
Gwen, a great recovery therapist;
Grand Junction, CO AA meetings that helped keep my sober;
Greg's mentors through the years: John, Ron, John, Jim, Loren, and Wes. Your work with Greg spilled over into my life and

helped me stay sober and live with emotional sobriety;

BEDI AA group in Aurora, CO for help keeping me sober;

Canyon View Vineyard Church, Grand Junction, CO Pastors and staff for support to allow me to lead Celebrate Recovery;

Canyon View Vineyard Church, Grand Junction, CO Celebrate Recovery Leadership Team—awesome men and women of God;

Heritage Christian Center, Denver, CO Pastors and staff for support to allow me to lead the Celebrate Recovery Program;

Heritage Christian Center Celebrate Recovery Leadership Team— awesome men and women of God;

Pastor Keith Boyer and Pastor Mark Hardacre for believing in me to lead Celebrate Recovery at Crossroads Community Church, Commerce City, CO;

Leadership Network, Dallas TX;

Leadership Institute, Commerce City, CO;

My sister Jenny and my brother Tom for your compassions through the years;

All the 1000's of women through the years that have shared with me their recovery;

My Children Stephanie (& Chris), Nick (& Melissa), Darren (&Chantielle), Justin, Charlie (&Heather) for walking this road beside me through the ups and downs; My Awesome Grandchildren Carson, Cole, Caden, Aubree, Cruze, Kaelin, and Braeden, for a better future because of my recovery:

I love you,

$\mathcal{D}$ianna $\mathcal{M}$ oore

Contents

Sponsors

Paul Rosenberg

Nick and Melissa Hanson

John and Linda Fields

Bill and Barbara Gibson

Jean Smith

Tamara & Eddie Olson

Foreword

GIANTS. We will all face them at some point in our lives. They could be external, internal, or most likely, both. Facing them is a given. How we deal with them is not. It's our choices in the context of our faith that will determine the outcome…*will we defeat the giants in our lives or will they defeat us?*

Greg and Dianna Moore have made some wise choices in facing their own giants. One of those wise choices was to write this book and put to print for the rest of us the wisdom they have gleamed from their personal experience.

Every joyous triumph and every painful disappointment are weaved into our life story. And until we reach the end of our journey it is often hard to see how each twist and turn, hill and valley are all a part of God's plan for our lives. It gives me great hope to know that God sees our entire lives from His unique perspective! It is also helpful to know that God never wastes a hurt. As we place our trust in Him, He promises to use it for good!

> *2 Cor. 1:3-4 (Msg) All praise to the God and Father of our Master, Jesus the Messiah! Father of all mercy! God of all healing counsel! He comes alongside us when we go through hard times, and before you know it, he brings us alongside someone else who is going through hard times so that we can be there for that person just as God was there for us.*

This book allows Greg and Dianna to come alongside you as they openly share about their personal battles, setbacks and victories.

I believe their transparency will help you face the giants in your life with purpose, hope and courage.

It is my prayer that through this book, you will come face to face with who God created you to be. That you will gain the tools you need in the battlefields of your life and that you will gain an understanding of the magnificent plan God has for you!

Keith Boyer

Lead Pastor, Crossroads Community Church

Introduction

I t takes courage to apologize and admit a mistake. It takes courage to be honest in a corrupt business world. It takes courage to fight prejudice. It takes courage to join 24 Hour Fitness, climb Mt. Everest, join AA, run the Boston Marathon, battle cancer or fight an addiction. It takes courage to stay in your marriage, to raise your children in the right way. It takes courage to swim against the current of political correctness. It takes a backbone to keep on doing what you know to be right.

It takes courage to… Face Your Own Goliath!

Much of what is perceived as courage is counterfeit. Like false gold it has no real value. In one form, what passes for courage is physical recklessness. Bungee jumping, alligator wrestling, and sky diving may be in this category. What about true courage? True courage is based on principles; whereas physical daring may be based on physical strength, on emotion, or perhaps hidden motives. An Ultimate Fighting combatant has physical daring, but why? Fame? Money? Mercenaries in the heat of conflict, gang members impassioned to kill, or confident because of superior resources, may display daring. However, courage is not based on superior physical power.

Facing Your Own Goliath takes mental and moral strength that comes from devotion to principles; Facing Your Own Goliath means tackling your challenges and overcoming your fear even though the outcome may not be clear; Facing Your Own Goliath takes faith, a self-sacrificing spirit, and a willingness to appear foolish while applying moral fiber, perseverance, and steadfastness.

It is not easy!

The Scriptures have described our times as "critical times hard to deal with..." To deal with them forthrightly takes courage. But, in a world where passing-the-buck is the norm, and placing-the-blame-elsewhere is a practice; how do we learn to face our own Goliaths? How do we practice kindness without victimizing ourselves or others in the process?

That is the purpose of this book! Courage has been described as "mental or moral strength enabling one to venture, persevere, and withstand danger, fear, or difficulty firmly and resolutely". So, where do we learn courage? When do we apply it? What if we fail? How do we pick up the pieces and try again?

This book creates the framework for understanding this daily human challenge. Whether we have a chronic disease, need a promotion, want to get married, or are deciding to go back to school; we must reach a decision. In our decision-making process, the precision and manner of it will determine how successful our results will be. We cannot, however, achieve our life-goals if we are unwilling or unable to...Face Our Own Goliath!

[1]

Goliath Roars ! How I Came Face to Face with My Giant: Greg's Encounter

I was born in Denver, Colorado, the middle of 5 children; and I felt lost in the shuffle. For me, the home was a place of vast emotional emptiness. I experienced my parents as physically devoted and emotionally absent. I loved them. I was sexually traumatized at a very early age, was acting out sexually by age 5, and furtively drank alcohol at family parties at about the same time.

There were many "Family Secrets" about drinking, sex, insanity, anger, and stories of affairs that I only understand as secrets in retrospect. What I learned was that we didn't talk about things or express emotions. This was to be done "behind closed doors", if it was done at all. I learned the skill of denial early and practiced it for the first 40 years of my life with increasing ferocity.

I was raised in a church going family. At 10, I answered an altar call and said the sinner's prayer. No one in the family spoke of this or offered any encouragement, except to ask, "Why did you do that?" I felt ashamed and embarrassed and never spoke of it again. I was given a Bible that I never read as I observed that no one in the family read or talked about the scriptures. Grace was for meal time and prayer only for bedtime. I concluded all the activity meant nothing.

At age 13, I was introduced to pornography and sexual acting out. My life took a marked downward turn. At 17, a promising athletic career was cut short by the start of my relationship with alcohol. I never got better in the ensuing 23 years; only worse. Bad Habits and poor character are progressive!

At age 18, I made a conscious decision to turn my back on "Church" and God. I walked away, not to return for 20 years! Even though I knew in my heart that God had a call on my life, my plan was better. Pride and selfish desires overcame everything else.

I went to a university, where I partied; "turn on, tune in, drop out, free love and more." I met my future wife in a 3.2% beer joint; alcohol was a common bond. When I graduated, we married and moved to the mountains. I associated with people who were like-minded in their pursuits of wine, women, song, thrill seeking, and orgies.

Over the next 15 years there was career success as I progressed to Executive Management in the resort industry and started a family with two sons. This obscured the reality of escalating, out of control behavior in my private life. We moved 20 times in 18 years. I was an expert in "geographic cures", always with the false idea that the next town or job would provide the answer to the problems I had created in the present location.

Each move added to the accumulating weight of baggage. Toward the end of this time, I was into murderous thinking, plotting to kill people as a way to end my misery. My sexual identity was confused. I was totally unaware of the insanity of it all. I only knew that I was angry, homicidal, and suicidal; nothing was working according to my plans at all. Narcissistic self absorption was killing me.

God sent some acquaintances that were concerned. They told me about the Lord, invited me to a Bible Study, and told me I was pouring my family's life "down the tubes" with my continuing drinking, drugging, and sexing. They also arranged for my employer to confront me and insist that my wife and I go to 12 Step programs.

They suggested AA for her and Al-Anon for me.

I suspect they knew I wasn't finished drinking yet!

We went and were introduced to recovery principles. This was the beginning of the Lord's work in my life. I didn't think I was powerless, but I thought that my wife was. I continued my behavior; my wife changed hers. In short order, I had behaved my way out of this job. We moved, again, this time into the basement of my parent's home as there was no where else to go. There ensued a long period of unemployment, initiating a further downward spiral and descent into pornography, drinking, and ever more severe depression and suicidal brooding.

This culminated in a moment in the basement of my parent's home with a gun in my mouth, thinking I would just "end it all" and "show them". In a moment of clarity, I realized that I didn't want my family to come home to find the mess. I determined to go out that evening, somewhere in the hills and do the job. God had other plans! My Mother-in-Law called and invited us to dinner.

That evening, as we sat in the lobby and waited for a table, the whole room went black. I was isolated, totally alone; unable to see anything around me. There was a beam of light streaming in, and a question impressed on my mind. I was asked: "Will you come to me?" This was a life or death question; would I choose life, or choose to die? I was frozen, speechless for what seemed an eternity. I realized I wanted life. I said: "Yes, Lord, I'll do it your way. I am terrified, alone, nothing is working. Please help me!"

Immediately, the darkness left. My family was talking away as if nothing had happened. I knew in my heart that something inside me had changed. I asked how long we had been there, and they said "About five minutes." I was aghast. I tried to tell them what had happened, and they looked at me as if I was certifiable! But I knew; I had met the Lord! That was April, 28, 1986.

Prior to this, I had joined a Bible Study. The man who was

leading the study reassured me, and suggested that I read through the Bible in a year. I was unemployed; I had plenty of time. The word came alive; it jumped off the page. I began to feel alive little by little. In about 30 days, I got a job: $3.30 per hour plus commission. I thought I had died and gone to heaven. We moved out of my parent's basement and into a rented place, made possible because the owner waived the damage deposit. Even though I didn't know what was happening, God's favor was upon me.

I continued attendance at recovery group, but drank occasionally, was troubled by lust and sexual acting out. My wife and I were growing apart, as she was pursuing a counseling degree and I was immersing myself in the Word. Our "world views" became increasingly disparate.

I was offered an Executive position in another part of the country. The boys and I went on to the new city. She determined that a divorce was her desire despite my pathetic pleading. I got very drunk the night the divorce was final. That was my last spree, August 8, 1988. After that, I stayed sober and was not drinking anymore, but life was miserable. I was in a new city, single parent with full custody, new job, no real support system. I really hit bottom this time, HARD!

Through the Recovery group, I repeatedly heard about denial, rigorous honesty, powerlessness, and sobriety. I was now at a point where there was a self-imposed crisis I could no longer postpone, evade, or deny. Through a boy's soccer team I coached, I met the Mother of one of the team members who was a recovering person herself. Her name was Dianna. She later became my wife.

Over time trust was built on our common interest in recovery. One day in the late fall on a walk, she confronted me about drinking, and asked "Are you an alcoholic?" I was stunned, as I had never allowed myself to address the question. I mumbled a response to evade answering.

Shortly after, my job ended abruptly. I was unprepared to handle a failure of this magnitude on the heels of a divorce. I was invited to a retreat weekend at the Church I was attending. On Saturday night, they had a "Confession" Service. As I entered the Chapel that evening, I knew there were only four words I had to say. I began to weep and sob uncontrollably.

I sat there, arguing with God. I was impelled to talk to the clergyman who sat waiting patiently. When I collapsed on the chair in front of him, these words came tumbling out; "I am an alcoholic!" That was all I could, or needed to say. Yet remarkably, I felt a cleansing that was truly transforming. I was speaking the real, honest truth for the first time in my life.

That was Goliath at that moment – a seemingly insurmountable obstacle. What was I to do? How would I summon the courage and power to face that giant? I did not know.

Greg

[2]

Goliath Roars ! How I Came Face to Face with My Giant: Dianna's Encounter

I am the oldest child of a family of three children. My mother was not married, living and working in Alaska, as a Public Health Nurse. I was conceived in a rape in September 1953. My biological father (To this day, I still do not know who he is and what my heritage is) was a Navy man on a 48-hour leave from his Navy ship. The ship ported in Sitka, Alaska where my mother would hang out in the bar with her nursing friends after work.

In December of 1953 my mother married my first stepfather. He was a very intelligent man who worked for the Alaska Airlines and was stationed in Sitka, Alaska. I was born June 20, 1954, Father's Day. How ironic, for I know my biological father knows nothing about me even today.

For 51 years, I was told that this stepfather was my biological father. This was a secret that was kept from me all those years. My sister, brother and all family members on his side knew this family secret. My mother did not tell her side of the family because of the shame of the situation. It was bad enough she was pregnant when she got married; how would it look if her husband was not the biological father, not to mention the shame about being raped.

So, I came into the world feeling rejected, feeling something was the matter with me and that everything bad was my fault. This emotion has been part of my whole life and much of the work I have done in my recovery.

My stepfather was an alcoholic. My mother was a "rageaholic" and extremely controlling. She used me as her scapegoat for her rage. To this day, I am still very frightened by other people's anger. My childhood years from 0-5 could be characterized by isolation, loneliness, rejection, neglect, fear, anger, emotionally absent mother, insecurity, physical abuse, emotional abuse, and sexual abuse by many adults in positions of trust.

At the age of 5 in September 1959 my mother got polio in her right leg. She was in a hospital in Seattle, Wa. My step-father (my sibling's real father) was taking care of us. He would leave us alone at night and for days at a time, go to the bar, tell us that if there was a problem to call the fire department and when the siren went off he would know it was us and come home.

His sister, my Aunt Millie removed the three of us from our home and tried to take care of us. However, it did not work out, so she placed us in The Johnson Home, an orphanage in Juneau, Alaska. Because I was in kindergarten I was separated in living quarters from my brother, Tom, and sister, Jenny. This separation theme, was and has been another element of hurt that has run rampant in my life and a huge hurdle in my recovery work over the past 22 years.

My mother was discharged from the hospital in February 1960 and picked us up from the orphanage and took us home to be together again. In July of 1960 my mother divorced my stepfather and moved us to live with our maternal grandparents in Iowa. My mother needed to heal from polio and started working part-time in a hospital in Waukon, 20 miles away. We lived there for one year and then moved to Waukon in the summer of 1961.

My mother had to work at night full-time and slept during the day.
My memories from ages of 5-10 were of my mom's rage, isolation,
unhappiness, loneliness, sadness, physical abuse and emotional
abuse by my mother and sexual abuse by my grandfather.

When I was 10 my mother married a man, my second stepfather.
His wife had just passed away and he had 3 children ages 15, 17, and
19. So we moved into his house with 2 of those teenagers.

At age 18 I married to get OUT OF THE HOUSE. This
marriage was characterized by anger, fear, lies, financial devastation,
mistrust, drinking, partying and more.

After 10 years of marriage I filed for divorce, was living on
welfare with three small children, went back to school and received
a diploma in a clerical program, and an AA degree in accounting.
I began a pattern of escalating drinking, partying, and sexual
escapades, most of which were dangerous.

During this time I had another purely sexual relationship with a
man, and yet planned to marry him. I moved to Dubuque, Ia., where
he lived, in August of 1985. I worked at a college in the Student
Services Office. While there I began to take classes.

I was a single mother on Iowa welfare, food stamps, living in low-
rent housing, with three young children ages 7, 10, 11. It became too
much for me to work and be in college, so, I transferred all of my credits
from the Junior College in Calmar, Ia. and went back to school full-time,
eventually earning a Business Degree in Business Administration.

Again, the pressure began to pile up. After an argument with
a woman in my apartment building, a friend suggested that I check
out some recovery group meetings as I was so angry much of the
time. Amazingly, I did.

That began a path that eventually led me to walk into a treatment
program, "Turning Point Treatment Center" in Dubuque, Iowa. There,
I had to admit that I had issues with alcohol and prescription drugs.

These were my Goliaths, and I was totally uncertain about how
to confront and conquer them.

Admitting my self to treatment was one of the hardest and best decisions I have ever made in my lifetime. I am thankful to God today for giving me the courage and strength then, to admit my problems and receive help.

After, becoming sober and gaining perspective on my life, I confronted another Goliath: my planned marriage. It had become evident that the relationship was not healthy for me. In July of 1987, I broke off that engagement and returned his ring. I had no idea what the future held, but I did what I had to do.

About Christmas time, my son Nick came home and said he had met this "really cool kid from Colorado".

In the spring of 1988, he came home from a teen recovery meeting (which I took my three children to every Sunday night) and said his friend from Colorado also was attending the meeting. I thought, "This is too coincidental."

That May, all three of my children joined summer soccer teams. I was to call a man named Greg Moore, as he was the soccer coach for Nick's team, the same team his cool friend from Colorado was on. I can still remember the night I called him and said who I was and why I was calling and at the end of the call I said "I understand my children and your children attend the same teen recovery meeting on Sunday nights.

By the way, who is the alcoholic in your house?"

A pretty bold question for someone I had not even met yet.

He told me that it was a family member, not him. I knew then on some level there was something in our future together.

I was holding on to sobriety, feeling shattered over the failure of my marriage and ensuing engagement, and uncertain about my / our future.

Goliath was roaring! Loudly!

Are you ready for a love story?

[3]

David and Goliath:
An Improbable Victory?

D o you recall the Hebrew Scriptures or Old Testament Biblical narrative about David and Goliath? Do you remember the thrill you experienced when first you heard the story of the shepherd boy defeating the giant warrior?

Perhaps it was magical. Did you envision, through the words of the Bible, a young man, boldly confronting an armored warrior over 9 feet tall with only a sling and a stone? Could he win?

As a youngster, my world was a small farm. Grandfather was a rancher, and he had a horse named Chief. He taught me how to ride. I have a vivid memory of mounting that horse from the top rail of the fence, proudly wearing my leather chaps, and remembering David riding out to defeat the Philistine armies. What a glorious vision!

However, that vision was short-lived as the cinch was loose, and the saddle, along with the short stature "cowboy" ended up on the alfalfa stubble; scratched, humbled, embarrassed. Giants are not defeated from that position! Grandfather said something very wise in that moment. He said, "Always, get back up on that horse that threw you." At that moment, there was not much "want to". I felt mostly hurt with injured pride. However, I mounted again, being sure to really tighten the cinch.

In the years since, there have been many grand visions of victory, and even more stinging setbacks, some defeats where all seemed lost, and times of terror, bewilderment, confusion, and despair. At those passages in life, the story of David seemed like a sweet fable that had no application to that particular *crisis du-jour*.

Perhaps, like we have, you have set off on a course of action, only to have something inexplicable, or an implacable problem, or an intractable person, block your way. Maybe it came from a source outside of you, maybe it arose within you. Wherever it came from, you wish it would go back to where it came from. Do you relate? There are "Goliaths", "Giants" out there.

Let's visit the story of David and Goliath to capture its essence and see what we can learn from it about courage and facing "Giants":

You will find the story in the Hebrew Scriptures or the Old Testament of the Bible, the Book of 1st Samuel, Chapters 16 and 17. This is paraphrased from the New Living Translation.

The story begins with one man's obedience to God's directions. It starts with an account of how the prophet Samuel was told by God to go to Bethlehem, to a man named Jesse, and to anoint a son of Jesse. This son God had selected to become King of Israel in place of King Saul. Samuel did as he was instructed.

Samuel did not know which of Jesse's 8 sons God had selected, only that it was one of them. The verses tell us the process. The very first son (Eliab) that Samuel looked upon, he said to himself: "Surely this is God's anointed man."

However, God gave Samuel some significant and important information. God said to Samuel: "Don't judge by his appearance or height, for I have rejected him." God does not make decisions the way we do! Most of us judge by outward appearances, but God looks at a person's thoughts and intentions.

Samuel looked at all seven of Jesse's sons that were present at that moment, and God said "No" to each one in turn. Samuel did not give up, but then asked "Are these all your sons?"

Jesse replied that there was the youngest, but he was out in the fields watching the sheep.

Samuel said to send for him, and awaited his arrival. When he arrived, God said to Samuel, "He is the one; anoint him." Samuel took the oil, poured it over David's head, and the Spirit of God came "mightily upon him" from that day onward.

Now comes the "Goliath" part of the tale. The enemy of Israel, the Philistines, gathered their army to do battle with the forces of Israel; the armies occupying opposite sides of the Valley of Elath between them.

Goliath, from Gath, is the Philistine Champion; a giant of a man 9 feet 5 and 3/4 inches tall! Imagine, 3 feet taller than Michael Jordan. His helmet and armor weighed 125 pounds. His Javelin was "as thick as a weaver's beam" and the head of the spear was iron that weighed 15 pounds. That is a heavy spear – heavy enough to pass right through an average 180 pound man. His shield was so big he had to have an armor bearer carry it ahead of him. Imagine this imposing figure.

The stage is set. Goliath considers himself invincible, as do his companions in the army. He issues a challenge. He is so certain of victory that he says: "Israel, choose someone to fight for you, and I will represent the Philistines. We will settle this in single combat. If your man is able to slay me, then we will be your slaves. But, if I kill him, you will be our slaves. I defy the armies of Israel. Send a man who will fight with me!" This went on for 40 days, twice a day; the giant strutting morning and evening, taunting the army of Israel.

Quite a proposition: Death or slavery – from the mouth of an undefeated giant!

Day in and day out they were reminded of their helpless and powerless state by their enemy. The passage says that Saul and the

Israelites were "terrified and deeply shaken."

Along came David. Remember, David has been anointed, and the "Spirit of God is with him." David's three oldest brothers have joined the Israelite army, and were with the army all the time. David, however, went back and forth between working for Saul (playing the harp) and tending his Father's sheep.

His Father, Jesse, sends him to the front with supplies for his brothers and their Captain. He also instructs David to bring back a letter from them about how they were getting along. Obeying his father, David set out early the next day. He arrived just as the armies were facing off across the valley, so he went forward to greet his brothers. As he talked with his brothers, Goliath came out from the Philistine ranks, shouting his challenge to the Israelites.

The Israelite army, having been taunted and terrorized, began to run away in fright. As they fled, they said things like: "Have you seen the giant? He comes out each day to challenge us." And, "Have you heard about the huge reward the King has offered to anyone who kills him? The King will give him one of his daughters for a wife, and his whole family will be exempt from paying taxes."

Notice a couple of things: The men were building up the stature of the giant in their minds, and the King was leading from the rear. He would not face Goliath, but was willing to pay someone else to do it. This fed the Israelite soldier's fear and bred mistrust as well.

David did something very astute. He talked to the men to verify the report he was hearing. He gathered facts, did a little on-site research. He asked "What will a man get for killing this Philistine and putting an end to his abuse of Israel? Who is this pagan Philistine anyway that he is allowed to defy the armies of the Living God?" Again he was told what he was hearing was true.

His oldest brother, Eliab, got angry as he heard David talking, demanding of David "What are you doing here anyway? What about the sheep? I know about your pride and dishonesty. You just want to see the battle!" In other words, he did his very best to put David "in his place" and to belittle him and his character; to dissuade him and to make himself look good in the process.

David was not dissuaded, saying to his brother "What have I done now? I was only asking a question." Then he proceeded to go to some more men and ask the same questions, and received the same answer. Several members of the army reported to King Saul that David was asking questions, so the King sent for him.

When David arrived before King Saul, he was talking to someone he already knew. What happens next is very interesting. David says to the King, the Commander in Chief, "Don't worry about a thing. I'll go fight this Philistine."

Do you think anyone would believe him? Would you?

No one did. King Saul, in our story, was incredulous. In other words, he was placed in a position of being asked to exercise belief without any track record to stand on. He did not see David as credible. To paraphrase him, "Don't be ridiculous! There is NO WAY you can go against this Philistine. You are only a boy, and he has been in the army since he was a boy." 'Who is kidding who? You have no track record in battle.' is the implicit question and statement.

David is undeterred. He says "I have been taking care of my Father's sheep. When a lion or a bear comes to steal a lamb from the flock, I go after it with a club and take the lamb from its mouth. If the animal turns on me, I catch it by the jaw and club it to death. I have done this to lions and bears and I'll do it to this Philistine too, for he has defied the armies of the living God. Jehovah who saved me from the claws of the lion and the bear will save me from this Philistine."

David makes a statement of fact about previous victories. He gives credit to God for the results, tells where the power comes from, and why faith is reasonable. He addresses King Saul's incredulity and declares that faith is the appropriate response. In effect, he says "I am credible." Back to the story!

Saul was disconcerted, but when he saw David's determination, he finally consented.

Saul then tried to be helpful. He gave David His armor, his personal armor. David tried it. He put it on and walked around a bit. He even took the sword and strapped it on too. He quickly concluded that he could not go out in the armor, saying "I can't go out in these. I am not used to them." So, he decided to take them off! (Can you hear the generals and soldiers snickering?)

Imagine the professional soldier's merriment when they saw what David did next. He went to the stream in the valley and picked up 5 smooth stones. 5 smooth stones – are you kidding? Then he stuffs the stones in his shepherd's bag. This boy has lost his mind! Then they know for certain he is certifiable when he takes his shepherd's staff and his sling and starts across the valley to fight the giant.

Picture the scene: two huge armies, a professional giant soldier, a young boy with a staff, a sling, and 5 smooth stones. You can hear the whispers.

Goliath emerged, with his shield bearer ahead of him, sneering with contempt at the boy. Goliath clamors: "Am I a dog that you come at me with a stick?" Then the story says, "He cursed David by the names of his gods." Next, he threatens "Come over here and I'll give your flesh to the birds and wild animals!"

Now, David has his say: "You come to me with sword, spear, and javelin, but I am coming to you with the name of Jehovah of armies, the God of the battle lines of Israel, whom you have defied. Today, God will conquer you, and I will kill you and cut off your head. And then, I will give the dead bodies of your men to the birds and wild animals, and the whole world will know that God does not need weapons to rescue His people. It is His battle, not ours. Jehovah will give you to us."

Notice the contrast of their lives: Goliath was concerned only for himself. David is concerned with the reputation of God and of Israel. David represents and speaks for them. He intends not to just defeat Goliath, but the whole Philistine army. David sees the bigger picture that Goliath's ego blinds him to, yet David does not speak one word about himself.

Goliath moves in for what he believes will be a certain, simple, and quick kill. Interestingly, David *RUNS* to meet him. David rushes to what to all appearances is certain death. He doesn't just walk. He doesn't sneak. He *RUNS!* One can reasonably suspect that Goliath was not expecting that! Imagine him pausing ever so slightly as he savored his sense of certain victory.

David, however, is efficient. He grabs one of the 5 smooth stones, sticks it in his sling, and engages the enemy. He hurls the stone from his sling toward Goliath and hits him, dead center in the forehead. The stone has such velocity that the Bible says it hit and "sank in". That stone was effective! Goliath stumbles and falls to the ground face down, immobilized, incapacitated.

Note; it is not the type of weapon David uses to defeat his enemy that is important. It simply takes any weapon, empowered by God in the hands of a willing servant. When capably aimed in the direction of the enemy it disables the "Goliath". David won with a stone and a sling – he had carried five smooth stones – he was prepared – but, God only needed one!

Since David carried no sword he runs over to the fallen "Goliath", takes the giant's own sword, and cuts off his head. It is interesting that the weapons of the giant proved the very thing that brought about his ultimate demise. What made Goliath seem invincible actually carried the seeds of his ultimate humiliation.

What happens to the armies?

When the Philistine Army sees that their champion, their invincible warrior, is defeated and killed, their courage evaporates. They turn tail and run. The Israelites, on the other hand are emboldened. They chase after and destroy the Philistine army and take their camp, weapons, supplies, and wealth as plunder.

There is more recorded. For our purposes, we will mine all that we can from this portion of the account. As we close the story, think about this:

David's triumph in the power and name of God emboldened his comrades. Selflessness and courage will always create trust and confidence in others and inspire them to greater heights, to join the battle themselves, to go after other "Goliaths". The Bible records in other verses, the stories of "David's Mighty Men", his "Inner Circle" of warriors defeating several other "Giants" that were relatives or cohorts of David's own Goliath.

Selfless courage inspires and emboldens others when they face their own "Goliaths". What you do or I do, like David, can be a key to victory for others.

Wouldn't you like to see others in your sphere of influence overcome their difficulties?

Your most beneficial service to those within your circle of influence will come through defeating your personal "Goliath". Thereby, those within your circle may come to know they too can Face Their Own Goliath and win!

[4]

The Samuel Effect: Anointing through Relationship

There are those whose lives are lived in such a manner they leave an indelible mark on our own. The character and influence of such people far outweighs the actual events they participate in with us. Samuel was such a man in David's life.

Who was the prophet Samuel? How did he come to such a position of influence that he was asked to "anoint" a future king? How did his actions have such a profound effect on David?

Samuel has an interesting story of his own. It is recorded in the Books of 1st and 2nd Samuel. Samuel was the son of Elkanah and Hannah. They were faithful Jews. Hannah was childless, and prayed to God for a son and vowed to give that son back to God as a Nazirite. Samuel was the answer to the prayer.

Hannah took him to the temple when he was young (possibly 3), and left him with High Priest Eli to serve in the tabernacle. Samuel's parents had an intimate relationship with God and were obedient to him. Samuel grew up serving obediently in God's temple.

The Scriptures report that God called to Samuel as he was

sleeping near the Ark. Samuel, thinking Eli was calling, got up and went to him saying, "Here I am. What do you need?" Eli said, "I didn't call you. Go back to bed." This was repeated two more times. The third time, Eli realizes that it is God calling Samuel and tells him, "Go and lie down again, and if someone calls again say: Yes God, your servant is listening."

Samuel goes back to bed, and a fourth time he hears "Samuel, Samuel!" This time he replies, "Yes, your servant is listening." God begins to speak to Samuel and from that moment on began Samuel's prophetic work. Eventually all Israel became aware that he was God's true prophet.

What is clear is that Samuel spent his life up to the time of his encounter with David developing loyalty and obedience to God; following directions carefully, fully, and immediately. He was the man who first anointed King Saul at God's direction.

When Saul disqualified himself as King, Samuel delivered God's words: "Obedience is better than sacrifice." Thus, loyal himself, Samuel came to anoint David to replace Saul.

Those like Samuel who live in Godly obedience, exert an uncommon influence upon those they encounter. Because they are steeped in truth, their actions and words carry a depth and weight that is unmistakable. You know who they are. You find yourself paying attention when they speak. Their influence is not based on charisma or machismo, but they lead by fine example, their depth of character is demonstrated in every day life and activities.

While we may not always welcome their words and choices, there is a certainty to them that we are inexorably drawn to. Our "Samuels" leave an indelible imprint on us, not because of the force of their personality, but because they carry God's spirit. As a consequence, if we willingly ask, God's Spirit becomes a dominant characteristic of us. While we may differ in temperament and behavior, their spiritual fruitage is passed on to us, influencing us for the good.

Their effect transcends who they are, as it is founded in a power source greater than themselves. The truth of their impact resides in their surrender to that power and in living it out in their moment to moment activities. They do not question what seems an improbable development. Rather they simply move into the tasks assigned, and trust that what they need to know to accomplish that task will be made known to them.

Obedient "Samuels" remain focused on each "assignment" until it is finished. They do not shrink back if at first it is not completed or it becomes more difficult and involved than they first thought. Their clear impact brings others into a new state of awareness and effectiveness.

Such was the case with David and Samuel. We see Samuel simply accepted a mission... As he went about the task of anointing a new king, he listened carefully to the instructions he was given, and did what was asked. What seemed obvious at first was in reality a teaching moment between God and Samuel.

God taught Samuel that He looks into our deepest parts, beyond our surface appearance to what is really in our hearts. Just as Jesse showed only 7 sons, to Samuel, it was the eighth, David, who got anointed.

David was not even thought of in the rush to be considered for the anointing by Samuel. Even his Father Jesse did not consider him until asked. This is not necessarily odd in light of the cultural norm of the day that required the eldest son to inherit the greater portion of the estate, and so on down the line. David, as the youngest would not ordinarily have been considered as he was 8th in line. God had a different plan.

Along comes "Samuel" bringing a different message. He says "I see you as God made you to be, not as who you appear to be now." No matter what our position "in line" God will fulfill his purpose . David's life was forever altered because of his encounter with Samuel. So it is with our "Samuels" today.

What if David had said "No Thanks" when he was sent for? He would have missed Samuel, the kingship, the "presence of God" and his date for victory over Goliath. Have you ever said "No thanks!"? Failing to answer the call to face our "Goliath" may cause us to miss the effect of a heaven-sent "Samuel" in our lives. We may remain frozen, powerless because we are cowed by the presence of our "Goliath".

Samuel anointed David and the "Power of the Spirit" came upon him. Who arranged the divine appointment placing "Samuel" into David's life? We know. God did!

Stop for a moment and think:

- Are there people in your life, now or in the past, who had that "effect"?
- Did you turn them away? If so,why?
- What were you afraid of?

Perhaps there is someone whose presence just seems to calm you. Perhaps they have uncommon wisdom, or speak truth, or some combination of all of these things which brings a brief respite from your "Goliath" roaring at you. Pay attention. These individuals may be your "Samuels" calling you to action.

Who has He sent to you?

- If there is no one, perhaps it is time to ask for God to send someone.
- As God does not wish that "anyone should perish", He will send someone if you ask.

- However, there is a condition: when He does send someone, you must cooperate with them and apply the fruitage of God's Holy Spirit.
- If you ask, receive joyfully.

David when asked, came, listened, was anointed, and the power of God came upon him. So it can be for us, if we ask.

Stones for your sling

Along comes our "Samuel" bringing a different message. He says "I see you as God made you to be, not as who you appear to be now." No matter what our position "in line" God will have his way and no one can prevent the greatness that God put in us from coming forth, except us.

[5]

Morbid Fear

Have you ever been "terrified and deeply shaken" by circumstances or people like Dianna and me? Have you ever been constantly reminded in some way of your failure or hopelessness? If you have, you know that it is a totally demoralizing experience.

Look at the circumstances described in David's story. Two armies, facing each other, yet no actual battle actions were occurring. We see a lot of posturing and "trash talking". Armies coming out each day facing off, Goliath hurling insults, the soldiers running away in fear, King Saul offering a reward – day after day for 40 days! No movement in any direction; everyone just "running in place". Lots of activity, but no progress!

Morbid Fear has two prominent elements: Fear of the Known, and Fear of the Unknown. Fear of the Known comes from what we experience, observe, and conclude from other people's results. Fear of the Unknown comes from our ruminating about possibilities that have not yet come to pass.

If you were a member of the Israelite Army facing "Goliath" what might this look like?

Fear of the Known

Goliath comes out every day, two times each day and hurls down his challenge. He is over 9 feet tall – a very imposing figure. Perhaps you are only around 5 to 5 ½ feet tall. He is nearly twice your size.

You know he is their champion. All your fellow soldiers are intimidated by him too. Your King, Saul, is reticent about challenging Goliath and tacitly admits his unwillingness to fight by offering a reward to anyone who will take the giant on. Based on what you know, there is ample reason to be fearful.

You have a real basis for Morbid Fear. You could die!

Fear of the Unknown

This arises as questions abound in your mind about the near and distant future. There are no answers, only more questions without answers. You find yourself continually thinking; developing scenarios about such things as this: What if we challenge Goliath and he wins? What if they don't keep their word and kill us instead of enslave us? What if we don't challenge him and people think we are cowards? Am I a coward? What will my family think? What will I think of myself? What do my friends think? What is the King thinking? What will my infantry officer do? What if I get killed? What if I don't get killed? When will this be over? What if it is never over? How long will this go on?

The thought cycle seems endless.

Another facet of Morbid Fear is that it freezes us in place, just as it froze the Israelite Army in its tracks.

During this "frozen time", we can also suffer from another form of fear that masquerades as prudence. It has been called "Analysis Paralysis". This form of fear is characterized by a demand for an endless flow of more data and information to "make a decision". Really, this is just a delaying tactic. It is a pernicious form of denial. Delay simply gives the enemy more time to prepare and solidifies our own fear.

Another temptation is to fantasize "Imagined Outcomes". We take what we know or believe we know and create catastrophic or cataclysmic outcomes in our mind. Then, we behave and make choices based on these paranoid thoughts. Because we choose out of a fear based construct, it is likely that we encourage the very results we are so diligently trying to avoid.

In essence, we sabotage our success and implement our failure. Thinking we are taking useful action, we are actually moving ourselves toward certain defeat.

As a result, we "fear the shadow of the dog".

Yes, Morbid Fear does that. It destroys truthful thought, sanity, dreams, people, armies, and civilizations. It is evil, corrosive, and deadly. Corrosive, it eats away the strength of anything it attaches to. Or, like a colony of termites, it does its work from the inside out leaving only a shell with no substance. Destabilized, we collapse in a heap, wondering all the while: "How did that happen?"

It is important that we learn to accurately distinguish between Appropriate Fear and the Morbid Fear we have been discussing.

What is Appropriate Fear? It is accurately related to a real, not imaginary threat. For example: When "Goliath" appeared, he was a real threat: he was large, well trained, and tested. It is normal to experience apprehension in such a situation.

Appropriate Fear is always a call to action: Fight? Flee? Duck and cover? For example: When approaching a cliff, fear is a call to take the action of stepping back; a prudent and reasonable response. Appropriate Fear is a path to realistic evaluation of possible outcomes and choice of effective response. It is geared to our wellbeing and continued existence.

Real Fear is rational. By that we mean that it generates a realistic and measurable response according to the need and situation. It is geared to solving the problem and removing the threat, whatever it may be. It is generally present-tense action geared to alleviate a real immediate or future threat, tactically.

In other words, Appropriate Fear stimulates timely, effective, measured, and sufficient action geared to remove or mitigate a tangible threat. David demonstrated this phenomenon by his actions that day as he went about the business of facing Goliath. Real fear could be described as "**Y**ou **O**bviously **U**nderstand **C**ourageous **A**ction **N**ow **D**etermines **O**utcomes" - **YOU CAN DO!**

On the other hand, Morbid Fear is radically different. As we have seen in our discussion, it has the opposite effect. Instead of calling us to action, it seeks to stop us in our tracks. Morbid Fear could be described as "**F**alse **E**vidence **A**ppearing **R**eal" - **FEAR**. While the emotional experience is similar, the thought process and resulting action is entirely different. So are the results.

Appropriate fear could be described as: YOU CAN DO!
"You Obviously Understand:
Courageous Action Now Determines Outcomes"

False fear could be described as: FEAR
"False Evidence Appearing Real"

Morbid Fear leads us to engage in the cycles we described previously. It leads to incorrect assumptions, thinking errors, ineffective choices, tentative action, pervasive disbelief, and ultimate defeat. Perhaps you, like us, have suffered from the debilitating and life devastating effects of Morbid Fear. The Israelite army was suffering from this syndrome until David arrived on the scene.

It is interesting to observe how both fear and courage are "transferable" from one individual to others and even to whole groups. Like a bad cold, fear is "catching".

A particularly virulent characteristic of fear is how fast it spreads. It may be more easily transferred than courage. Fear only needs imagination to do its dirty work. It spreads as an unstoppable virus, quickly and with deadly effect.

Courage, to be transmitted, requires evidence of its work in both mind and action; in tangible results. The wonderful thing is its power. Just one instance of heroic courage can completely exterminate Morbid Fear. True courage triumphs over fear.

David's courage motivated a whole army, as we will see.

Stones for your sling:

Courage triumphs over fear like the rising sun conquers the night.

[6]

Games We Play

Once more to the story of David; Samuel had to anoint a new person to be King because Saul had disobeyed a direct command from God. Saul then tried to cover it up, denying his true motives of greed and jealousy. For this and other reasons he disqualified himself as King.

Remember what God told Samuel. "Don't judge by his appearance or height, for I have rejected him." God does not make decisions the way you and I do! We judge by outward appearances, but God looks at a person's thoughts and intentions, all in the proper context.

In other words, it is not just what we say or do, that really determines who we are. Our core character is most likely hidden deep in the recesses of our heart where no one, not even we ourselves can see.

Most of us have several "Faces" we wear as needed. One we present to the world; "great Dad", "perfect Mom", "Business Executive", "Beautiful Person", etc . One we wear for ourselves; the "I'd like to be _____" or the "I think I'm_____". Another underneath it all – is who we really are when no one is looking: the "I lie", the "I'm jealous", the "I'm hurting", the "I can't stop". Like in ancient Greek tragedies, we wear masks. They serve a potent role in our moment to moment existence. We have carefully developed these to protect ourselves from both a predatory and emotionally damaging world.

In order to wear these masks, we have to tell ourselves and the world "out there" stories about them. We invent characters they represent and give them various attributes necessary or convenient for each purpose. The difficulty arises when we become aware on any level that the characters we present do not square with the internal truths of who we really are.

Thus, we develop another convenient survival tool, "disconnecting from our internal reality". We create a pretend world of motives and experience that match the masks we wear; we enter a delusional existence of our own creation. We construct untruths that we carefully rationalize and reinforce by persuading others to believe them as well.

It is clear our masks have their genesis in our self-protective thoughts and intentions. Truly our hearts are the seat of motivation and therefore we must "safeguard" them. Not wanting to fool ourselves, we need to examine our hearts, and see what God finds there. If we do not, we are subject to "torment", even as Saul was, when he left God.

What happens when our Goliath/s arrives? All those feelings, situations, past and present experiences, and hurts that have been long postponed or evaded suddenly shout their presence in a deafening roar.

Our very own "Goliath" has made himself known. He is blaring across the Valley, about his impending, total victory over us. His intention is to destroy us!

If you are anything like us, you cower in terror, feeling desperate, bewildered. "Is life worth the struggle?"

The things that we began doing as "protection" for ourselves; the masks and denial eventually develop into patterns of behavior that have unintended and often devastating results. While we never set out to walk into trouble, that is precisely what we do anyway. In order to continue to maintain our 'masks" we engage in all forms of deceptive behavior, lying mostly to ourselves, denying our real motives.

As a consequence, we morph over time into choices and actions that bear little resemblance to the person who began the journey. We may find ourselves saying and doing things we said we would never do.

An "innocent" flirtation becomes an adulterous affair, one drink becomes twenty on a regular basis, a "small" lie leads to a string of falsehoods that threatens our livelihood, a first glance at illicit photos becomes a lifestyle of degradation. Each of us could increase the list with relative ease using our own experience if we are even a little bit honest with ourselves.

We feel that we dare not change or the whole "house of cards" will come down and we will be found out.

As we continue in this way a pervasive sense of futility and hopelessness invades the spirit. We can no longer manage the "Goliath" we have unleashed into our lives. It is at this point the truth becomes evident that we are powerless over our behaviors, emotional pains, habits, and even our addictions. Our "Goliath" begins to assert itself.

Perhaps there is a question for which you have no answer, a "Goliath" with no name. Maybe there is a battle between you and another about who is responsible, or what is true between you. Which "Goliath" has the power?

There may be a battle in your mind about what the truth or reality of your situation is. "Goliath is shouting his challenge! Days, weeks, even months and years may roll around and find you seeking, (but not finding) trying to fill a hole that is bottomless. The fear of "Goliath" is demoralizing you.

Relationships may lie shattered along the path of your life, bringing gut wrenching pain, terrible loneliness, and dreadful endings. You may even have a Love-Hate relationship with your "Goliath". We know, we've been there!

The reality is we cannot overcome these things by our own power. Our best thinking has led us here. We have to somehow come to terms with this fact, and admit we are powerless by ourselves over our "Goliaths".

We must wake up!

What do you need to admit?

A Behavior you can't stop?

An Addiction? A compulsion?

A hurt you can't forgive?

Abuse of some sort?

Trauma?

Someone else's affect on you?

Fear of_____?

Failure of some sort?

Stones for your sling:

What is the name of your Goliath? Whatever it is, write it here. Name your "Goliath" as clearly as you can:

[7]

Preparing to Face Goliath: Asking for Help

Join with us as we now realize we cannot make changes by our own power. Neither could the Israelite Army. We are terrified of our Goliath and want to run away. We have, like the soldiers in the Army, built this "Goliath" up in our minds to the point that we are helpless in the face of it. We have enlisted others to do our battle, and still remain stuck with our "Goliath".

We recognize there is a valley to cross, and it seems too wide and deep, and the giant on the other side is too big. Now what?

Remember David? He comes along with a fresh perspective. He hears the same "Goliath" ranting and raving and says "Who is this guy? Does he think he can defy God and get away with it?" That is a legitimate question for us: Whom are we believing; "Goliath"? Or, is there someone else we ought to listen to?

Where can we, like David, gather some information about our battle? What exactly is it that we have been missing? Clearly, like David ignored his brother, Eliab, it is likely that the "friends" that we have been listening to are already defeated in their minds, even as we may be.

What we need is readjustment, balance.

We will need to listen to some "outside" counsel like David did. There is help to be had if we will seek it out. A well prepared, caring Godly person is often able to see what we cannot. She/he is able to help us get a sense of proportion and perspective that we lack. Do not hesitate to avail yourself of such assistance. It is an entirely beneficial exercise of humility.

Coming to this point of admission, understanding our common experience of defeat, what now?

You may be asking:

If not me, and what I have been doing, then what do I do?

What is to be the basis of living?

If not my thinking, then whose thinking will it be?

If our own carefully crafted systems of belief are crumbling beneath their own weight, where are we?

Notice what David did: he turned to God. He began to praise God. He began to recount God's blessings and mercies. When he went in front of Saul, he talked about God bringing him victory over the lion and bear. He gave credit to God, and said that the power comes from God.

Let's examine this more closely, as clearly, our thinking needs to be re-adjusted.

Clearly, when we are disturbed and without internal peace, there is something amiss with us; something out of kilter, off balance, needing adjustment. We are the problem! We may liken ourselves to an off balance Whirlpool Washing Machine that rattles, clanks, vibrates noisily, struggling to accomplish a task made even harder by the dissonance inside.

Clearly, when we are disturbed and without internal peace, there is something amiss with us; something out of kilter, off balance, needing adjustment. We are the problem!

The proposition that our thinking is somehow distorted in ways we are only at this point dimly aware of is disturbing. We may be downright panicky in our reaction to this dawning reality.

A sense of impending doom may lurk nastily, stealthily planting the thought that we dare not proceed, there is too much at risk.

None of this is true, but we may feel it to be so. "Goliath" has us convinced, yet we are aware that he is likely lying to us. We can no longer function with or believe the lies of "Goliath", but are afraid not to believe them at the same time. What are we to do?

Over and over again we go around the barn, hoping that the next trip around will take us to a different destination even as we tread the same path. Just like the Army of Saul, we may sit for "40 Days" listening to our "Goliath".

We profess surprise when we end up in the same place, in front of the same barn. We choose a familiar place, even though it is extremely painful. We accept the familiar pain, rather than confront the disparity between our illusions (fantasies of expected results) and the reality of our outcomes.

Our next steps may come swiftly or haltingly, but they are certain to come. What direction will we choose?

David's response was to recount the victories his God had given him. He spoke of the external power source as he went about fighting the wild beasts. He recognized that he had not done this on his own, and said so.

We can imitate David's course for practical application. Sane thinking is simply making decisions based on truth, staying connected to things and ourselves as they are. We can choose David's power source. We can choose God!

The idea we need to be restored to balance, like the errant Whirlpool, may not sit well at first. In fact, we may outright reject the notion. Even as Saul and the Israelite Army did not believe they needed help, we think we don't either. David knew better.

How do we "get it", the truth that we need to alter our thinking?

How's our current thinking working out? Are the results we have, the outcomes we want?

Did King Saul and the Army believe they were doing the "right things"? Did their results say otherwise? Didn't they think running away would get them out of difficulty? Didn't the exact opposite occur?

Does your own story yield this same nugget of truth?

Sanity may be defined as "soundness of mind; making decisions based on truth". Would you say in the examples cited above there was sound thinking going on? Had "Goliath" twisted the thinking of Saul and His army? Had anger and fear driven them? Had their thinking led them in a positive direction?

**Consider the following as you ponder
the quality of your own thinking:**

- Do you have a struggle identifying what is falsehood and what is truth?
- Perhaps your ego is raging out of control. Are you demanding answers before even knowing what the question is? Do you want the solution before defining and working the problem?
- Are you among the walking dead? Looking, yet not seeing; hearing and not comprehending; walking but not moving. Are you broken from the beating that life is administering?
- Is confusion spreading its evil tendrils in your mind?
- Are pride and selfishness destroying your relationships?
- Are discouragement and thoughts of suicide occupying your mind?
- Are you feeling like a lost sheep?
- Do you live in fear of death?
- Do you struggle with the idea that you need help?
- Are you willing to consider that you need a power source outside of yourself?
- Are you willing to believe?

Whom will you serve?

Eventually we come haltingly, or running, to the inescapable fact that we must have help from a source outside of ourselves. Like King Saul and the Israelite army, we have been battered (or maybe just fear what we see coming) to the point that we are willing to try a different solution. We have begun to see that pride and illusion have kept us trapped, and now we become willing to change our beliefs.

Stones for your sling:

It is a basic principle that when we are disturbed and without internal peace, there is something amiss with us; something out of kilter, off balance, needing adjustment. We are the problem!

Two things become paramount:
First: Acknowledgement that there is a Power greater than ourselves.
Second: We must have help from that Power if we are to live.

What are the elements of your battle?

[8]

The "Courage Compass": Foundation for Action

So it is, we must now move on. How?

To challenge our own "Goliath" requires courage. To take on a "giant" that has been taunting and terrorizing us calls for action that we, perhaps, do not have tools for yet. To prepare a foundation for thinking about such action, let us consider the "Courage Compass".

For ease of illustration, think of a magnetic compass. We orient to true North, where the magnet needle always points, and we can go to each compass heading as needed, always orienting relative to true North. So it is with courage.

> **North:** Spiritual Courage
> **East:** Moral Courage
> **South:** Emotional Courage
> **West:** Physical Courage

Let's consider each "Compass Heading" in its turn.

David, guided himself oriented to true North, Spiritual

Courage.

David was "anointed" – set aside for God's work
David believed God was with him.

We conclude from his example vs. the Israelite army:

- We are powerless in the face of our "Goliath" and that our lives are unmanageable in regard to the "giant".
- We realize that we need a source of power outside of and greater than ourselves to face and defeat the "Goliath".
- We recognize we need to be "plugged into or come into a relationship" with, a power in the person of God.

For our purposes of thinking about the "North" of **Spiritual Courage**, how does all this tie together? We suggest it lines up this way:

Each of us can choose to be like "David – a giant killer". Each of us can choose our path whether "Oriented to North" or elsewhere. Each of us can accept proper orientation from God. His Spirit supplies the power – if we are obedient to it – that propels and sustains us along our Compass heading.

In other words, spiritual courage comes from God. It is his power that supplies what is needed. We do not have to muster up courage on our own; it flows to and through us from Him.

Consider again the words of David: "**Who is this pagan Philistine anyway that he is allowed to defy the armies of the Living God?**"

David was exhibiting "spiritual courage". Notice what he did not say. He did not say "Who is this man that he defies us / me / you?" No, he said: "**Who is this pagan Philistine anyway that he**

is allowed to _defy the armies of the Living God_?" **(Italics mine).**
It is clear that David understood where the power resides, and was
giving expression to the reality of the situation. That is how "Spiritual
Courage" is always manifested.

It happens when we express in our actions, bowing to "God's
Spirit" and honoring God's power, God's will, God's position. It is
the beginning and ending place.

Let's continue.

Consider a Compass Heading of East: **Moral Courage.** Moral
Courage could be defined as willingness to stand for the right thing
because it is the right thing. Another term we may use is _integrity_.
The Hebrew words meaning "integrity" come from a root word
expressing sound, whole or faultless actions.

Let's hear David again:

"Now his oldest brother, Eliab, got angry as he heard David
talking, demanding of David "What are you doing here anyway?
What about the sheep? I know about your pride and dishonesty. You
just want to see the battle!" In other words, he did his very best to
put David "in his place" and to belittle him and his character; to
dissuade him and to make himself look good in the process. Do you
know anyone like that? Perhaps even done that to someone else?

David met resistance; he was not dissuaded from what he knew
to be right. He was as un-affected by other people as the truth (what
is right) is un-affected by people's opinions.

David continued gathering information from those around him.
He understood the nature of the situation accurately. Moral Courage,
by nature, looks for the right thing by looking past the opinions of
people to ascertain the truth. It moves to the side of truth rather
than trying to twist the truth to a more popular or politically correct
position.

When David arrived in front of King Saul he in effect said:
"Don't worry about a thing. I'll go fight this Philistine." Moral
Courage says: I'll stand on this ground because it is the right thing to

do. David had **Moral Courage**. He was Oriented to North; Spiritual Courage and heading East to Moral Courage!

Now then:

Let us move on to Compass Heading South: **Emotional Courage.**

Emotional Courage describes the internal discipline to take appropriate action despite what our emotional state may be telling us. Bravery is "doing it though afraid" so to speak. This is not to be confused with reckless disregard. Emotional courage is a sober determination to do the right thing in spite of our emotional imbalances at the moment.

Think about David talking with King Saul about his determination to defeat Goliath. The story clearly reveals that David has the measure of self discipline needed to face the task at hand. The last sentence is revealing: "God who saved me from the claws of the lion and bear will save me from this Philistine." David clearly states his experience and reveals his emotional makeup at the time. How many of us would do the same today?

David clearly has a source of confidence that does not come from his own abilities. One of the interesting things about courage is that when we are spiritually "oriented to north", our purposeful life's course comes into proper perspective. That is plainly demonstrated here.

David's ability to face "Goliath" with emotional courage is confirmation of his proper spiritual condition. His foundation is unshaken by circumstances. He can focus on the task at hand with serenity of heart because he knows where his power comes from.

We have the same source available to us. We must rely on that power source, to "look" in that direction instead of ourselves. Situations can deceive us if we are relying on our own power. Each of us has a sense of our own capabilities, limitations, and memories of past defeats and humiliations.

The tendency is to view new challenges through that lens, or to replay that tape. As a result, our feelings follow our beliefs and experiences of the past. Thoughts of failure and impending doom will seek to invade our consciousness when we are face to face with our own 'Goliath".

The beauty of "orienting to spiritual north" is that it allows us to readjust our thinking, while noting: "I can move ahead in faith and trust because the power to overcome does not rest in me alone. It flows to and through me from God. Therefore, no matter what my emotions are in this moment, I can speak and move forward in confidence."

Our emotional selves may kick and scream, telling us, "It's not safe!" However, the truth is as David declared, God gives the victory. We can be emotionally stirred up, and yet be assured at the same time.

Emotional Courage is the power to face and defeat "Goliath". It comes from a source that is always available, present, flowing, and greater than any situation or giant that we may face. Trust that power, not yourself. Remain "oriented to North."

Think now about **Physical Courage,** "West" on the dial of the Courage Compass. **Physical Courage** is the arena where we calibrate the headings and prepare to engage in appropriate action.

Simply doing the next "Right Thing", or if there is not clarity, doing the "next thing right" are varieties of physical courage. There may be great risk to our physical well being, or only a little. In any event, we can learn from how David approached his task of facing "Goliath". Let's review this part of the story:

David makes a statement of fact about previous victories. He gives credit to God for the results, tells where the power comes from, and why faith is reasonable. He addresses King Saul's incredulity and declares why faith is the appropriate response.

We are considering Physical Courage. What did David do?

- He set his jaw with determination.
- He let people offer their assistance.
- He evaluated his options for armor and weaponry, and chose what he could use.
- He gathered ammunition - the best he could find.
- He gathered what he needed for his journey.
- He took the first steps and then kept going!

Real Physical Courage is not characterized by bravado and recklessness. It is demonstrated by sober preparation utilizing previous experience, learning, teamwork, and effective strategy. It is always based on a sense of "mission and purpose" that rests on our "North Orientation". It is accompanied by Moral and Emotional Courage as companions.

While Bravado and Recklessness may show a willingness to take physical risks, they are really more a demonstration of our foolishness than anything else. When we happen to come through unscathed, we may attribute that to courage. Perhaps it was only athletic/physical ability. This form of success may lead to a spectacular defeat very quickly as we become more emboldened and self-assuming with each victory.

Our pride leads inexorably to a great fall. Such was Goliath's experience. He got cocky, and paid dearly for it; so will we.

History is replete with examples of men and women who have had similar "Goliath" experiences. Each quickly learned that lack of preparation, poor planning, and bravado combined with a big ego is a disastrous combination.

Courage is not the word to describe such situations; foolhardy is a more apt comparison.

On the other hand, examine the "David Model":

- Sober preparation utilizing previous experience

and learning
- Effective strategy
- Full speed ahead execution

Physical Courage is not a "stand alone" activity. It is founded in the "North Orientation" of Spiritual Courage", is supported by Mental and Emotional Courage, and involves each of the "David Model" activities.

Consider the first element:

Sober preparation

David did not launch out without first looking to previous situations for instruction. In other words, he evaluated what he had and knew what would be applicable to the current battle. He also evaluated his present situation and determined what he could effectively use. He planned ahead. Then he gathered what he could use, being very selective to gather only the best that was available to him.

David worked with Saul and his Army. He considered their input and proffered assistance. He chose that which was suitable for his mission.

He recognized that while he was going to fight the giant alone, he was not alone in the battle. Big difference!

Effective Strategy

David thought through how he would engage the "Giant". He had a battle plan already prepared in his mind to guide his actions. He carried what he needed to execute the strategy, and had extra "ammunition" in the form of stones. He had his weapon, the sling, with him, and took his staff to help him steady himself as well as serve as a backup weapon if needed.

Full tilt action

David, having prepared, planned, and equipped himself as well as he could, then stepped into action. He headed in the direction of his "Goliath" fully prepared to engage.

David, depending on his God, was spiritually oriented.

He was mentally in the right state of mind; he was emotionally stable, and physically prepared.

- How about you?
- How will you:
- Reorder your spiritual life so you are rightly related to God?
- Change your thinking about the nature of your "Goliath"?
- Develop emotional stability in the face of what seems an impregnable difficulty, person, or situation?
- Prepare for action in an effective way?

The answers to these questions will allow you to determine how to reset your "Courage Compass" to "Face Your Own Goliath!" We will examine how to address these questions next.

Stones for your sling:

Spiritual Courage is manifested when we express things, through " God's Spirit" in terms of "God's power, God's Battle, God's position. It is the beginning and ending place.

Moral Courage could be defined as integrity.

Emotional Courage is taking appropriate action in spite of what our emotions may be telling us.

Physical Courage is the arena where we combine the headings and prepare for and engage in appropriate action.

[9]

Evaluating your "Compass Headings" Part 1: Taking Stock of Ourselves

To answer these questions in an honest and realistic fashion, we need to look at our character. Think about this for a moment. We each have several personas we present. We present the persona we want others to see; the persona that we tell ourselves we are, and the persona that is truly who we are when no one else is looking.

In order to really answer the questions, we will have to honestly come to terms with three key facets of our character. These three facets are crucial to our "David" character; our own internal makeup which will determine how we orient for battle with our "Goliath".

Each Facet is represented in either David as an asset, or Goliath as a deficiency. On one side of each aspect is a character asset; the other side is a character defect. Each in turn will lead to either an effective way of thinking or an ineffective one. This in turn results in actions that lead us toward dealing with our "Goliath, or running away in defeat. Since our topic is "Facing Goliath" examine these traits.

Asset – Deficiency Sets:

Set 1: (David) Unselfishness/Humility/Honesty

or

(Goliath) Selfishness/Pride/Dishonesty

Set 2: (David) Trust/God Reliance/Courage

or

(Goliath) Self Reliance/Fear/Cowardice

Set 3: (David) Self Control/Considerate/Healthy Relationships

or

(Goliath) Self Absorbed/Inconsiderate/Unhealthy Relationships

Take a look at each set. As was stated earlier, assets and deficiencies are binary. One is selfish or unselfish; prideful or humble; honest or dishonest.

Similarly, we can be trusting or fearful; courageous or cowardly; Self reliant or God reliant. We will exhibit self control or self absorption; consideration of others or disregard for them; damaged relationships or healthy relationships.

While there is a continuum or spectrum of possibilities in each facet, we are always moving toward one or the other. We cannot move toward honesty at the same time we move toward dishonesty. In that regard, they are mutually exclusive.

How do we accurately identify each characteristic in ourselves, and then devise a plan to develop the positive and reduce the negatives? In order to be better positioned to confront our "Goliath", we must develop the internal strength of character to do so. This means we must take a deeply honest and thorough look at ourselves.

Here are a few suggestions about how to proceed. Do not shrink from what may at first glance appear as an unnecessary activity.

Ask yourself these questions:

- Am I getting the results I want utilizing my current thinking, actions, and beliefs?
- Is my "Goliath" defeated?

If your answers indicate any shade of "no", then uproot your deficiency, and cultivate the corresponding assets.

All of this is grand theory, but is useless without a practical actionable plan that is readily implemented. For a plan to be effective, it must be implemented fully. If you choose to follow this path, make a commitment to follow the trail to the end. Stopping in the middle is an invitation to failure and even greater difficulty at the hands of your "Goliath".

On the other hand, if you endure to the end, like David you will conquer.

Consider each set in turn, beginning with

Set 1: Unselfishness/Humility/Honesty as evidenced in David, and
Selfishness/Pride/ Dishonesty as evidenced in Goliath.

Begin with David

How did he evidence these Character traits? Back to the beginning of the Story: David was tending his Father's sheep when Samuel arrived. He unselfishly continued to perform his duties. He went to visit his brothers when his father sent him on the errand. He responded to the insult to God, and not to the ones to himself. He was honest with King Saul about his purpose and did not overstate his experience or his abilities. He relied on God for strength and for victory. He put God first. In short, he exhibited unselfishness, humility, and honesty.

Goliath was boastful, arrogant, cocky, self reliant,

egotistical, and self serving. Pride was his mainspring, as he was the "champion" of the army. He was so certain of victory that he did not even stop to honestly consider the possibility of defeat. His self reliance was so supreme that he even used the names of his "gods" to curse David. Goliath was so confident within himself that he dared to use his false "gods" names in a manner that directed the credit to him instead of them; a dangerous tactic to use in any circumstance.

While we all know the outcome of the story, it is easy to dismiss Goliath as a fool.

However, how many of us would be able to so casually dismiss these things if the spotlight were on us? For example:

- How have you been dishonest with yourself or others?
- When have you sought to make yourself look better than you really are or were in a given circumstance?
- Have you taken credit for something you did not do?
- How has pride led you to dismiss your faults and exaggerate the faults of others?
- Have you disregarded others in your headlong pursuit of your own agenda?
- Have you denied your part in difficulties with other people; perhaps even the bigger part?
- Is the fault generally with others and not with you?
- Have you set situations up to ensure you're looking good regardless of what happens to other people?
- Do you experience resentment toward others?

We could go on. Very few, if any of us could answer positively to such questions. In fact, it is likely that even a cursory, superficial answer to such questions will reveal there is much that could be considered as deficient. We each have much of "Goliath" in our makeup in this regard.

Let's examine

Set 2: Trust/God Reliance/Courage as we see in David

and

Self Reliance/Fear/Cowardice that is in Goliath.

David first

He acts in a consistent manner through out this encounter. He speaks of God first and always in a manner that reveals he trusts God to provide for his needs and to give him victory. He is very clear about where his power source is, and indicates that he is relying on God to come through for him each time. His courage is rooted, not in himself, but in the total certainty God will be victorious in and through him. In simple terms, David realizes his purpose is to serve God wholeheartedly, not himself.

Now consider Goliath

It is easier to appear courageous when your physical stature is as intimidating as Goliath's was. Brute force is more often a symptom of fear than courage, especially when it is aggressive and offensive in nature as was the case here. Real courage is always contained and directed, not just thrown out indiscriminately.

Self reliance, in this case, is demonstrated by Goliaths utter failure to give credit or acknowledge anyone other than himself. His power, as he understood it, arose from within himself and was surely sufficient to meet the challenge as he saw it. Self reliance always causes us to have a distorted perspective of the totality of a situation. We are limited to what we know or can do, and there is always someone or something bigger than we are. Defeat is inevitable, as Goliath clearly experienced.

Some questions to ponder in this regard:

- What we trust in is revealed by our actions. What do you trust in, really?
- What are your fears (specifically – name them)?
- What are you trying to postpone, evade, or deny?
- What is your power source?
- Have you been able to overcome your fears on your own power? (Hint: if you still have the fear, you have not been able to overcome on your own power.)
- Has self reliance failed you?
- How could you plug into a greater power source?

Set 3: Self Control/Considerate/Healthy Relationships;
and
Self-absorbed/Inconsiderate/Damaged Relationships?

David, in the narrative of the story, clearly demonstrates self control. He is focused, clear about his values, intent upon his purpose, and clean and clear in his actions. That is self control at its best. He is considerate of his father, his brothers, the army, the King, and most importantly, his God. His relationships are characterized by respect, humility, honesty, and forthrightness.

Goliath

While we have no record of interaction with his army, we can see that the story clearly indicates he was full of himself as evidenced by his rantings toward the Israelite Army and toward David. It is impossible to be selfish and not be inconsiderate toward others. After all, when we are the center of the universe, what else really matters in our world? Goliath clearly did not consider David a person worthy of anything but disdain and mockery. He was used to being served; he even had an armor bearer to carry his shield. He was so egotistical he did not even see the need to protect himself fully. His relationship with his own army was so fragile that they fled rather than defend his honor by fighting when he was defeated.

A few questions for evaluation:

- Where have you been selfish, dishonest, or inconsiderate in your dealings with others?
- Have you inspired mistrust or bitterness in others?
- What was your real motivation: Self or selflessness?
- Do you engage in transactional relationships: give to get, you do for me and I'll do for you or vice versa?
- Do you disguise this as helpful, love, or serving?
- Are you a grudge holder?
- Do you find that you move from relationship to relationship, regardless of the nature of the interaction (friend, lover, business, acquaintance, etc.)?

While we may all want to be like David in character, it is likely that we have some "Goliath" traits that we need to purge. What is paramount at this juncture is to recognize the exact nature of our deficiencies so that we can move toward gaining victory over them.

Stones for your sling:

Recognize that assets and deficiencies are mutually exclusive.
While there is a continuum or spectrum of possibilities in each facet, we are
always moving toward one or the other.

What is paramount at this juncture is to recognize the exact nature of our
deficiencies so we can move toward finding victory over them.

[10]

Evaluating your "Compass Headings" Part 2: Resetting the Compass Heading

Having made this sobering evaluation as honestly as we are able, the next question we have to squarely confront is, "Now what?"

Goliath waited too long and completely lost any opportunity to change course. Let us learn from his example and determine to do whatever it takes to change course.

The first lesson to learn from the story is this: David clearly knew in his heart where his power came from. We would do well to emulate his example. Think about this: if we could have overcome our deficiencies on our own before this, likely we would have. Consider the common Toaster. How well does it work if it is not plugged in? You can put bread in it, mash on the button, and wait.

Without power, it looks good, seems to function, and yet produces no results. So are we when relying on our own power; lots of activity, looking good, great effort, producing mediocre results. There is no lasting change, just as there is no toast. Just bread!

These "course corrections" involve the need for substantive changes in our character. This means core changes of our beliefs, thinking, and consequent actions. Simply "resolving" to do better will not suffice without readjusted actions to support the effort.

So, we have to have help from outside ourselves. Our own resources are insufficient to effect the necessary changes; to make course corrections that are sustainable. We are like the stale bread. How do we plug into the power to access what is needed to effect the change we seek? We identify what is deficient in ourselves.

Return again to David for clues. David relied on God for everything. When he needed strength, he knew God would provide it. When he was assigned a task, whether it was to guard the sheep from lions and bears, carry greetings and provisions to his brothers, or battle Goliath, he put his confidence in God, not himself. His strength arose from his relationship and trust in God, not from overt confidence in his own abilities.

As a practical matter for us, we can proceed along this course:

- We can admit our flaws.
- We can recognize that we need to exchange selfishness for selflessness, self absorption for God consciousness.
- We can humbly go to God and ask him to remove these deficiencies in character and replace them with his own spirit and power.
  - » We can seek for unselfishness, humility, and honesty.
  - » We can operate in trust, God reliance, and courage.
  - » We can exhibit self control, consideration of

others, and develop healthy relationships.
*   We can go and do the next right thing, confident the needed power to do the right thing will flow to and through us.
*   To the extent that we seek to carry out God's will and lay down our selfishness we will encounter, as David did, the power to conquer our internal and external "Goliath".

The end result is an orientation of our internal compass to "Spiritual North" with the accompanying mental, emotional, and physical courage to "Face Our Own Goliaths." Our internal compass accurately directs us: helping us to become "God – willed". Our Lives will revolve around God, moving in constant step with Him.

Stones for your sling:

We have to have some help from outside ourselves. Our own resources are insufficient to effect the necessary changes; to make course corrections that are sustainable.

Following this thinking in our own situation means if we wish to have more of the facets of the character of David, and diminish the facets of Goliath, we will have to seek God and request he work in and through us.

[11]

Leveling Out: Setting Matters Straight

Having arrived at this juncture, we need to look toward the future. We are preparing a foundation for a new way of living and approaching the "Goliaths" in our lives. In addition, and even more precious, is the fundamental change that is occurring within. It will bear fruit in our lives, and in the lives of everyone we encounter.

Part of building this foundation involves a straightening out process in ourselves. Another vitally important building block is our relationship with others.

It is a prominent feature of David's relationships that he did not have any enduring conflict with other individuals or groups as recounted in the story. He really did not even have a conflict with Goliath as a person. He did however, have a conflict with the principles that Goliath represented.

This is a crucial distinction. David focused on the *principles inherent in the situation, not the people involved and their personalities.* Consequently, he was free to take the necessary action unfettered by personality differences. Substance was the issue, not style. He did not get hung up in non-substantive issues that were outside of his objective.

For examples regarding people and personality:

- He did not let the issue of style of battle gear interfere with his mission to defend the name of God.
- He did not let his brother's accusations deter him from gathering needed information.
- He did not permit the enemies taunts to affect his thinking or his demeanor.
- He did not seem to notice the reward that the troops said King Saul had offered to anyone who could defeat Goliath.
- All of the items listed above are matters of **personality traits and personal preference.**

Regarding principle:

- He did focus on past victories that God had given him.
- He did focus on determining his best strategy, tactics, and armament.
- He did submit to the authority of the King.
- He did determine clearly why he was entering the battle and knew who gave him the power and the victory.
- All of these matters are matters of principle.

His "Compass" was properly oriented. The result was a

noticeable absence of conflict as he went his way. He was single minded about defending the name of God in his thought, emotion, action, and spirit and consequently was empowered by God. The result was victory.

Consider Goliath:

His whole demeanor shouts of focus on personality rather than principle.

- All of his taunts were aimed at denigrating other individuals and groups of people.
- His boasts were all about himself.
- All his parameters for victory were couched in terms of ensuring that he maintained the personality of "champion and conqueror."
- He mentions his "gods" to use their names to curse his opponent, not to honor his "gods". What a demeaning use of their names.
- He was also narrowly focused – on himself. He was concerned with self aggrandizement, personal glory, enhancing his stature, and maintaining his position.
- All of these indicate a focus on people at the expense of principle.

He was full of self reliance and personal power. He does not mention anyone other than "Goliath". The result was defeat and death, not only for him but for all in his army,

We can either be a David, or a Goliath, depending on how we choose to focus and act. Focusing on Principles energizes us to face Goliath in God's power. Focusing on Personalities diverts our energy into non-productive activities. One way leads to victory for everyone we are in relationships with, the other to defeat for us and those in our "army".

- Which will we choose?
- How will you answer?
- Will you move to the side of truth?

Since we are considering "leveling out" there are some issues to consider:

- Perhaps, by our actions, we have affected and / or redirected the course of other people's life in a negative direction.
- Future events are unknown and to a large extent uncontrollable, so we likely will face circumstances, "Goliaths" that will seek to "disorient" our compass.
- We may choose to be truth centered and principle oriented, or pride centered and personality oriented.
- We have determined there are principles, traits of character that we need to develop and activate to live more effectively.
- It is certain most of us have left "human wreckage" in our wake, even as "Goliath" did. It is imperative we seek to "level out" personally and set matters straight with those we have damaged in our pursuit of self interest.

What is the next indicated action for us? How and why should we even consider this proposition of "setting matters straight"?

If you are familiar with the history of David, you are likely aware that after his triumph over Goliath, things deteriorated quickly between David and King Saul. In fact, King Saul spent years trying to kill David out of jealousy. Saul made no effort to set things right in himself or between him and David. Relationships can turn on a dime if issues are left to fester and are not addressed. Such was the case here.

Setting that aside, let's consider some hypothetical questions: What if David had let his brother's accusations distress him? What if he had gotten angry with King Saul for suggesting that He use the King's armor? What if David, out of resentment and bitterness toward his Father had refused to go to the battlefield that day? None of these things happened, but what if they had? The outcome would have been significantly different.

What if King Saul had refused to honor his pledge to reward anyone who would fight and defeat Goliath? What if David's father had disparaged David and not sent him to check on his brothers? What if David's brothers had resented his staying home and sent him away before he heard Goliath? None of these things happened, but what if they had? Would the outcome have been significantly different?

Clearly, the quality of relationships in any situation has a significant impact on the outcome of events. Therefore, creating and maintaining the best possible relationships would appear to be in the best interests of everyone. Great ideal! Unfortunately, our selfishness, pride, and self seeking get shoved back and forth between us and others creating untold damage. The Bible calls this sin.

Call it what you like, it is a fact we have all experienced hurt at the hands of other people.

Call to mind an event which left you smarting at the hands of someone else. Perhaps that person came later and said "I'm Sorry" and then proceeded to hurt you again. Maybe they have hurt you repeatedly. What ever the case, it is probable that as a result of being victimized you have a pervasive mistrust of people. You probably experience bitterness of heart which transfers into interactions with others unrelated to the person that damaged you.

Perhaps you find you are jealous of others who haven't suffered as you have. Perhaps there is resentment; you can't seem to "get over it". All of this is simply to illustrate that damage to people created by actions of others is real and pervasive. Since we are now about the business of setting ourselves to face the "Goliaths", these are the first "Goliaths" to consider.

Here is a simple course of action to follow that is logical, consistent with our objective to conquer "Goliath", and readily implemented.

There are two components to this:

1. Forgive those who have harmed us.
2. Set matters right with those we have harmed. Forgiveness is a principle. So is making things right with others.

This is the place where we begin to focus on principles, not people and their personalities. As we learn to do it here, it will carry over into every other area of our lives.

What exactly do we do?

It is very difficult to set matters right with others if we have not set them right within ourselves. That is where forgiveness comes in.

Consider the following:

- Forgiving others involves the past but affects our future.
- Forgiving frees us from the emotional bondage to the hurt.
- Forgiving does not mean we are saying what happened is OK or acceptable.
- Forgiving does not mean we have to continue or

reestablish a relationship with another person.

- Forgiving does not mean we have to trust someone who is not trustworthy.
- Forgiveness does mean we are trusting God instead of ourselves. We are rightly "oriented".

Forgiveness is a grand concept, we have all heard of it, and yet we seldom really practice it. Why? Generally it is because we receive little instruction as to practical steps that we can take to effectively do it. Hurt and damage to our psyche and emotions do not go away simply because we wish they would. There are many practical suggestions about how to take action to enter into forgiveness and make it a part of our character. (Go to roar@ recoveryandredemptionpub.com for a list of some ideas.)

You have completed the first phase of "making things right", the crucial part of straightening out your internal life. Now, let's consider how we can do the same externally in our relationships with others.

Now, we must do everything we can to set matters straight with those we have hurt, even as we have seen how others hurt us. This is also a principle. Our mission is to get our life in order so we may be without hindrances to moving forward.

Even more importantly, by doing so we will position ourselves, as David did, to meet great challenges and be of maximum benefit to those around us. We will go from being a distraction to others to being an asset in their lives.

In order to do this, we will have to take another look at our past actions from a different perspective. Most of us do not have real difficulty in identifying how others have hurt us. However, many of us have no realistic assessment of how we have affected others.

In order to make things right, we need to examine where we may have been wrong in our actions toward others. We are preparing to confront our own character defects in a practical way and address our impact on others.

Ask yourself this piercing question: "In any of my relationships have I been selfish in any way?" If so, to whom, and when were you selfish? Be as ruthlessly honest with yourself as you possibly can. Think of a few words to describe how you were selfish, dishonest, or uncaring and inconsiderate towards this person. You are trying to see how you may have hurt and damaged them.

It is imperative that we do our utmost to make it right. Ask this question about the situation: "Will making a personal overture to them create further damage to them or their relationships?"

Now, you are prepared to take the next action; actually talking to those you have hurt. This is a simple and straight forward process, but it must be handled with utmost care. Our purpose is to clear our side of the street. We will not engage in any discussion of any one else's choices or behavior. We stick to our own "stuff".

See   roar@recoveryandredemptionpub.com   for   specific suggestions and directions. Note the following carefully:

> DO NOT make such overtures or amends to anyone who will be further damaged by your doing so. We are not to buy our peace of mind at someone else's expense. Here is a rule of thumb: When in doubt, don't.

Here is the bottom line: You are now free to move forward without any constraints from the past regarding damaged relationships that have been left unattended. Goliath will begin to seem less unconquerable now. You now know how to straighten out relationships, because you have experienced it in your own life!

These principles are expressed in the Hebrew and Greek scriptures as found in the Bible. In recovery programs such as AA and similar organizations, these activities are built in as an inherent and integral part of the process as they set it forth. We all are indebted to them for their pioneering of these principles in a practical, applicable, and effective manner.

Stone for your sling:

Another vitally important building block is our relationships with others.
A crucial distinction is to focus on the *principles, not the people and
personalities.*

Forgive those who have harmed us.
Set matters right with those we have harmed.

Will you move to the side of truth?

[12]

A New Center:
Continue What You Have Begun

For our lives to have true purpose, we must whirl around our God. And if we do, we are properly oriented at all times. This is the type of life orientation we are seeking to develop. We will have an accurate "center". What relevance does "A New Center" have for us?

We concluded in Chapter 9 that our Courage Compass will have a central role; that we will revolve around God. An extremely accurate type of compass, a gyrocompass, always points to magnetic "North." It always points to north no matter what position it is in – it inherently orients properly. "Gyro" is a Greek root word that means a circle or a combining form that is a "circular or spiral motion; a whirl". God is our "true north" that we circle around and toward which our compass should always point.

Look to David's actions as he continued what he had begun and see what we can glean from it regarding his center, his "compass" (Reread from Chapter 2 if you wish to refresh your memory). Let's consider:

He starts across the valley to fight the giant.

- He is equipped, prepared, and properly oriented.
- He voices his faith; he declares where the power comes from, and whose victory it is: God's.
- He sees the bigger picture.
- He moves assertively.
- He activates his weapons accurately and fully for maximum effect.
- He continues the battle, taking advantage of strategic and tactical opportunities.
- He stays engaged until the victory is complete over the "Goliath".
- He set the example for others, they followed his lead.

This pattern certainly is worthy of emulation. Having properly prepared and oriented, David "Faced his own Goliath".
SO CAN YOU!

Let's consider each in order:

- He starts across the valley to fight the giant. He is equipped, prepared, and properly oriented.
- Have you done the work suggested previously?
- Is your life circling, swirling around your relationship with God? Is your "gyrocompass" in working order?
- Have you "named" your "Goliath", identified it precisely? Have you admitted to yourself that "Goliath" exists for you?
- Have you consulted with others who have fought

similar battles and learned what weapons are most effective?
- Have you practiced using your weapons?
- Do you have a support system, your "army" to back you up (at least one more person who will be there for you)?

He voices his faith; he declares where the power comes from, and whose victory it is: God's. Will you:

- Speak, that is; declare audibly, words of faith in God?
- Do you believe He is the power that moves you?
- Understand that the battle is God's and you are an instrument in His hands?
- Know that no "Goliath" is bigger or more powerful than God? Victory is certain, only timing is unknown.

He sees the bigger picture. When engaging the enemy:

- Your battle is not just for you.
- It will be a demonstration of God's power for others to see!
- They will learn from your example and freedom will spread.

He moves assertively. David ran to meet Goliath. Will you run to meet yours?

- Having determined to confront your own "Goliath" you must move ahead determinedly and assertively.

- Action is no longer optional, it is mandatory.

He activates his weapons accurately and fully for maximum effect. David used a stone and a sling. What will you use?

- Your "gyrocompass"?
- Honesty, thorough honesty?
- Truth in your relationships?
- Trust God to lead you in the way you are to go?
- Develop your character?
- Change your playmates and playpens?
- Choose different paths?

He continues the battle, taking advantage of strategic and tactical opportunities. How can you stay engaged so you can:

- Pursue the tactics you have started?
- Ask others to support your efforts? Form helpful alliances?
- Pursue new opportunities for growth?
- Develop or use other weapons / methods that reinforce your efforts?
- Make your initial efforts stronger by using them consistently?

He stays engaged until the victory is complete over the "Goliath". Have you and will you:

- Thought about what victory over your "Goliath" will look like?

- Determined to stay at it until you experience release?
- Go to any lengths necessary?
- Be as fearless and thorough as you can be?
- Persevere through whatever it takes?
- Be willing to do these things for the long haul?

He set the example for others. Do you understand:

- Others are watching?
- You are a leader by virtue of the battle you are leading in your own life?
- Your victory is important?
- Your influence is vital?
- Your character matters?
- The inspiration you are to others has lasting impact?

They followed his lead. Be ready to:

- Have others ask for guidance and mentoring.
- Be challenged to walk new and greater paths.
- To be led into deeper pain and surpassing joy.
- To become ever more aware of your deep need and dependence on God like David.

The "Compass of Courage" we began the chapter with serves as an orienting methodology resulting in victory for us and inspiration for others. Our "New Center" can and will have great impact in our "world" as we "Face Our Own Goliath".

Stones for your sling:
Our New Center serves to:

Ensure we are equipped, prepared, and properly oriented.

That we voice faith; declare where the power comes from, and whose victory it is: God's.

We see the bigger picture.

We move assertively.

We activate our weapons accurately and fully for maximum effect.

We continue the battle, taking advantage of strategic and tactical opportunities.

We stay engaged until the victory is complete over the "Goliath".

We set the example for others.

Others have the chance to follow the lead.

[13]

Expanding Effectiveness: Grow in the Victory

David's triumph in the power and name of God emboldened his comrades. Your selflessness and courage may create trust and confidence in others and inspire them to greater heights, to join the battle themselves, to go after the "Goliaths".

There are two words in the above statements that are keys; Selflessness and Courage. These are hallmarks of David's character as evidenced in this specific story recounted in the Bible. They are also the very things we are seeking to develop and build into our lives as we "Face Our Own Goliath". The opposites of these two traits are Selfishness and Cowardice.

We will either go forward, or backward. There is no such thing as remaining static in the spiritual arena. Healthy things grow. We may go dormant for a period of time. If we go dormant, the normal process is to come out of dormancy and continue growing.

Dormancy can be a hopeful state if the purpose is to rest for a period of growth and to consolidate previous gains. Prolonged dormancy in living things, without emerging, eventually leads to starvation and atrophy. Ultimately, we must grow or die. The choice is always ours to grow or not. However, the manner in which growth will occur, the mechanism of it, the circumstances, will often not be our selection.

This increase of effectiveness is the result of a deliberate placing of our lives under the care and control of the true God. The certain result is a stretching, refining, and polishing process that will be anything from mildly uncomfortable to deeply painful.

It is however, pain with a purpose, and will most certainly be the precursor of a deep, abiding, joy; a fruitage of God's spirit.

We have identified the "Compass of Courage". We have mentioned "A New Center". Let's take some time to consider some of the elements and perspectives that are involved, and how we can foster our own growth and that of others.

The Compass of Courage began with orienting properly spiritually, and then moved to mental, emotional, and physical courage. We fleshed out the concept with the addition of circling and revolving around God in all things. God is our magnetic north, so to speak. This produces the power and preparedness to confront our "Goliath" and move into a new way of viewing life and its challenges.

This "New Center" encompasses:

- **Our Spiritual To Physical Orientation**
- **Our Mind Over Heart Choices**
- **Our Major vs. Minor Impacts**

To "encompass" something means: to include without exception, to contain, to surround, and to circle around. No matter which direction we look, these components are always a factor in our "compass heading;" our direction of travel.

Each of these was present and active in the life of David, and of necessity, must be present in our life as well if we are to maximize our usefulness.

Our Spiritual to Physical Orientation

In the discussion of the "Compass of Courage" it became evident David put spiritual things first. The physical action always followed those dictates; never preceding it.

Our New Center includes these two elements in every circumstance. This will lead us to more fully grasp the chain of events, evaluate the options, perceive potential consequences, and make effective decisions.

A way of thinking about this is as follows: A creator creates an object, using physical materials, to represent a thought or concept formed first in thought. For example, the pottery is the result of the thought in the potters mind. The object embodies the thought, but is not the thought. The reality of the thought gives rise to the reality of the object.

Our Spiritual Orientation gives us clear perception of the truth of God that is inherent in our situation. Real truth is not relative; it exists in its own right independent of physicality because it originates in the mind of God. God's truth determines the appropriate response. Our orientation to God produces the ability to accurately assess circumstances and situations in our moment to moment existence.

Our thinking will begin to move along these lines:

- What truth of God is operative here? What Spiritual principles are inherent (represented / symbolized) in the physical circumstance I am in?
- In light of those principles, what action or response is indicated?
- What Physical activity will best implement the

principle?

- What meaning or consequences will naturally flow from appropriate or inappropriate actions?
- What will serve God's will for us best?

Each time we engage in this, we develop a fuller comprehension of both the Spiritual and Physical content of life and situations.

As our experience grows, our understanding grows, and thus our effectiveness increases. It is a never ceasing process that can only bring benefits to us and others.

The good news is that even though we try and fail, God only asks that we recognize and admit our failure, and then that we get up and once again do our best. He will do the rest.

Another piece of good news is that we can reduce the volume of consequences that fall on the negative side of the ledger. While we cannot eliminate them entirely, we can do the best we can to improve our results. We can strive for progress. We cannot earn grace, but we can benefit from it and pass it on as best we are able.

Selfishness will cause us to seek our physical and emotional preservation instead of seeking God first. Selfishness is oriented to the physical, is devoid of understanding, and is usually destructive in consequence. To the extent we selfishly pursue our own ends, harm is done and destruction results. We cannot ignore God and get away with it.

Selflessness is developed in our surrender to God and his will. Selflessness is energized as we see Spiritual truth and principles and act on them.

Courage blossoms as we; face our own mortality, choose to act with the truth and principle in mind, take action to do His will, and stand for truth. This means that as we follow God, good can be served, and benefits can accrue. That is a good deal by any measure.

So it is; we must do God's will. This is the heart of all truth.

Without it, as we have seen in our own lives, nothing of value is forthcoming.

- Which will we choose?
- What boundaries will we set for ourselves in service of this reality?

Mind Over Heart Choices

While our emotions are God given and immensely valuable to us, they are not meant to be our decision making apparatus. Having made a decision to follow God, the course is set. Consequently, we need to seek the "mind of God' in all matters and dedicate our heart to follow that course.

We will inevitably run into our own emotions and predispositions which may be counter to what God would have for us. Inheriting sin, it is likely our life, our mind and heart, will never be free of this conflict. However, when we plug into a new source of power, our God, we can do the right thing. In fact, we may grow to the place where doing the right thing will be the only thing we consider.

We will learn that our emotions preceding a decision, while an assistance to us, are never as useful as those that follow when we do the right thing. In fact, it is the emotional resolve which follows our actions that bridge us to further positive action.

From it we glean understanding. This is different from temporary pleasure which is fleeting and subject to our momentary whims and physical state. Joy springs from a source beyond us and is given to us as a gift from God. Its value is immeasurable.

The companion of Joy is peace. By peace, we do not mean the absence of conflict. Instead, we are in synch with God and no matter what the external outcome, our course is certain. This produces a clarity of thought and action which cannot come any other way.

Instead of being overcome by circumstances, we stride through them with a calm heart and clear, purposeful action. Even when we are not certain of what action to take, we can pray and be certain we will be guided and provided for as we move forward.

Major vs. Minor Impacts

Consider this series of events: A young man is sent on an errand; he arrives at his destination; he overhears a warrior boasting; he asks some questions; he decides to defend the name of his God; he goes before the King; he prepares a plan; he takes action; he defeats the enemy; soldiers are emboldened; the army is routed; God is glorified down through the ages.

It is a likelihood that David did not start out on his trip to visit his brothers with eternal impacts on his mind. He was simply doing as his father requested. However, as we see from this summary of the chain of events what happened had major impacts. What is true for David is true for us today. Seemingly innocuous situations may have long term significance.

Keeping our compass oriented to "spiritual north", as David did, will position us to exert the best possible influence and can result in great impact, for a long, long time.

In other words who we are and what we do matters; there is no such thing as insignificance.

- Will you be whole-souled, whole hearted, and mindful?
- Or will you be soulless, halfhearted, and mindless?
- Will you accept and act out of your significance?

Selfishness diminishes us, others, and our impact.
Selflessness seeks to strive for the greatest impact, on the greatest number, for the greatest good.

Obedience, like Samuel demonstrated, lays down our personal agenda in favor of serving God's purposes and is linked to major impact to others and God's world.

Our "New Center" matters! Your "New Center" matters! Anything else is the ultimate deception. You are a unique creation; the result of 1 in over 8.5 million possible combinations! There is no one else who can do what you can do, who can have the impact you will have! **YOU MATTER!**

Just like David, you can be a Giant Killer. You were made for such a time as this; to "Face Your Own Goliath!"

Stones for your sling:

<u>Selflessness</u> and <u>Courage</u> are hallmarks of character and are the very things we are seeking to develop and build into our lives. This is the result of a deliberate placing of our lives under the care and control of God.

Who we are and what we do matters; there is no such thing as insignificance.

Will you be whole-souled, whole hearted, and mindful?

Or will you be soulless, halfhearted, and mindless?

Will you accept and act out of your significance?

[14]

Motivate the Army: Give as Freely as You Have Received

We have discussed how what you do has an impact on others.

David's triumph demonstrates this phenomenon wonderfully. Here is a plausible scenario:

The armies are watching David and Goliath carefully. As David's battle unfolds, the Generals in the Israelite Army shout; "Get ready, whatever happens we need to be ready!" As the armies see the giant go down, the command goes forth; "Weapons ready!" When they see David grab Goliaths sword and dispatch Goliath, a wave of disbelief, then relief, then courage sweeps through the men. The order comes to the advancing soldiers; "Charge!" They are already on the way. No one needs to tell them the obvious: "We will win today!" *The battle is already won, only the clean-up actions remain.*

So, your "Army", those in your circle of influence, will be affected. Your influence is likely greater that you believe.

Consider:

- The average person directly exerts great influence on 5 – 7 people.
- Each of those people has the same number; you influence people who will influence people. We are now at 25 – 49 without even working at it.
- Take that out even 1 more level and you reach 125 - 343.
- That is just direct influence. Think about the sustained effect of a changed life over time. Think about the possibilities of the power of association. People become like the people they spend time with. Your "Goliath" victory and the subsequent growth in you will plant seeds in others lives that will grow over time.

What is interesting to observe here is influence was "caught – not taught". That is to say, David led by able example and in so doing others "caught" the "victory vision" and took action themselves. David didn't make speeches, develop systems, teach about being proactive, or any other such thing. Empowered by the Spirit of God, he simply observed the need, calculated what he had to fight with, shared his experience, stated his faith, and took action – capable action.

God inspired action has an effect unlike any other activity. Because God is at work, there is an energy that is uniquely attractive and instructive at the same time. People are drawn in and lifted up and they often don't know why. But they will generally be led to inquire about the experience. Real truth does that!

As a victor, you are the bearer of the flame. Your victory has within it the spark which can light the candle for others. It is crucial you understand it is not you; it is the example of your victory and the Spirit within you that is at work. You simply carry the message; a very profound message.

As a victor, you become an influencer whether you are aware of it or not. Influencers have that effect because they do what others haven't or won't. They have made choices which everyone faces, yet not everyone will choose the path of facing Goliath.

Change occurs in groups of people in discernable ways. In this case, David was an instrument of change. The status quo was that the armies sat facing each other, hurling insults and challenges, but not moving anywhere. Along comes David. He takes action and the whole situation changes. Everyone is moved to action in some manner. Like a mobile, when one part shifts, everything else has to move to achieve a new place of balance.

So it is with you. You do not have to have a grand design. Simply go forth and confront your "Goliath". In the "slaying of your "giant" you plant the seeds of change for all those around you. Good seed cannot bring forth anything but more good.

Know this; your life is forever changed. You will no longer be able to comfortably stay in a place of willing subjugation to circumstance. You have been shown the path to confront challenges successfully. The path you travel will likely be that of continuing opportunities requiring increasing trust and faith. Many of these may appear in a seeming negative form. Be comforted. This is a certain affirmation of your growth and increasing capability.

Never hesitate to give away what you have freely been given. Life lessons, principles, your actions, the impact of others, experiences, all are yours to give away. The tide raises all ships. Your tide of well doing, coupled with the growing well-being inside you will not only raise your "ship" but that of all those around you. How wonderful is that?

Simply by "Facing Your Own Goliath" you are in the mold of a "Davidic Warrior". You are acting as a leading influencer in your realm. Thank you for making a difference. Thank you for BEING the difference. As you live, remember who you are. Look toward what you will become! Do, as David did, accomplish the next right thing in front of you to do!

Stones for your sling:

What you do has an impact on others. It is crucial that you understand that it is not you; it is the example of your victory and the Spirit within that is at work. You simply carry the message. You will no longer be able to comfortably stay in a willing place of subjugation to circumstance.

The Resurgent Goliath: Self-Assurance

David won a great victory that day over Goliath, and many more in the months and years that followed. There were trials as he fled from King Saul who plotted for years to kill him. Eventually, after King Saul was killed in battle, David did become King of Israel as Samuel had anointed him to become.

Then, as we are all apt to do when we have had a victory or a string of victories, he let down his guard. He forgot where the power that had produced the victory flowed from. There is a great lesson for us contained in this.

Let me paraphrase for brevity sake another portion of the Bible, 2 Kings, Chapters 11 and 12:

David is King of Israel. It is spring. Instead of going with the army, David sends His General, Joab, and the army out to fight. He stays in Jerusalem at his palace.

He naps one afternoon, and afterward goes for a "stroll" on the roof of his palace. He sees a beautiful woman, Bathsheba, bathing. He inquires who she is, and is told she is married to one of his soldiers. He sends for her anyway, brings her to the palace, sleeps with her, and sends her home. She is pregnant as a result, and sends him a message letting him know of this fact.

David responds by ordering her husband Uriah home, hoping that he would sleep with her and thus cover David's tracks. Her husband refuses as his loyalty to his comrades and God precluded living a life of comfort while his companions are suffering. He did the honorable thing.

David then sends a letter with Uriah to deliver to the General that orders General Joab to place Uriah in the front lines and pull back so he will be killed. The General does so, and Uriah is killed. David plays dumb when the report of the action comes to him.

Bathsheba mourns for the required time. Then David sends for her, brings her to the palace and she becomes one of his wives. She gives birth to a son, yet the Bible records "God was very displeased with what David had done."

God now sends Nathan the Prophet to confront David. Nathan tells David a story that contains the basic elements of his adventure with Bathsheba in a different form. David becomes angry and says "Any man who would do such a thing deserves to die! He must repay four lambs to the poor man for the one he stole and for having no pity." Then Nathan delivers the "coup de grace" and says "You are that man!"

Nathan then goes on to deliver the verdict of God and the consequences which will come to David as a result of his actions. In the course of this pronouncement, Nathan conveys this message "Why have you despised the Word of God and done this horrible deed?"

After hearing all the consequences as a result of his actions, including the death of Bathsheba's son, David confessed "I have sinned against God." Nathan replied that "Yes, but God has forgiven you, and you won't die for this sin. But you have given the enemies of God great opportunity to despise and blaspheme Him, so your child will die." This is the important portion of the story for our purposes.

What happens when we become self assured as David did? Self-assurance undermines our dependence on God, on the power that brought us victory over our Goliath. In fact, it increases the possibility that another "Goliath" will arise to challenge us.

Even as we exert positive influence in victory, we exert destructive influence in our self-assurance, our self seeking. Our lack of vigilance in maintaining our victory may hurt others.

Consider:

- Bathsheba got pregnant out of wedlock.
- Joab was complicit in murder.
- Bathsheba became a widow.
- Bathsheba's son dies.
- Constant threat of violence comes on David's family.
- His rebellious son publicly sleeps with David's wives.
- His rebellious son is killed.
- What David did in secret, his son does in the sight of all Israel. Public disgrace is complete.

A lot of destruction flowed from David's lapse. We would do well to learn from this. One victory over a "Goliath" does not ensure another one if we forget it is our relationship with God that empowers us. Our move to independence from God will always have devastating consequences for all who are even remotely involved.

David got complacent. What if he had prayed before he sent for Bathsheba the first time? What if he had gone to battle with the army? What if he had asked God for direction instead of "despising the Word"?

Here is an important point: when David confessed, God forgave him, but did not relieve David of consequences. Disobedience has a fee. Our choices have consequences for us and others. Even a cursory glance at our world today will reveal example after example of this chain of events. On Wall Street: Big businesses and bankers all created victims. In Religion: pedophile priests, greedy televangelists, and lewd Pastors are forced out of the pulpit in an orgy of media coverage.

Vigilance in maintaining our connection with God is the only path to avoiding this pitfall. Humility, remembering our state before "Goliath" and seeking God in all things are remedies for weakness.

The moment we think we can decide what is right, we are wrong. At that precise moment we move into a position of "playing God", taking upon ourselves a role God has reserved for Himself. We will never come out on top in such an endeavor.

Our place is to "treasure the Word of God", follow Him, and not our own self-deceiving ideas. David followed his desire and sowed destruction. He forgot the precious nature of his relationship with God and acted accordingly.

Our desires spawn more "Goliaths".

- Why continue to repeat the pattern, "going around the barn" one more time to end up at that same place?
- Insanity could be thought of as doing the same thing over and over expecting a different result.
- Do you want to continue the: victory followed by defeat followed by regrouping to fight again cycle?

God's ideas always work; ours do sometimes. Resolve to move deeper into your relationship with God so that you do not have to fight the same "Goliath" again and again. You will grow, and others will be spared destruction.

Should you choose to go your own way, the odds are 100% you will be right back where we started this book, facing a "Goliath". Then you will again have to clean up the wreckage, set matters straight, and then battle the resurgent Goliath.

This "Resurgent Goliath" may look different in appearance, and be even more daunting than the last one. This is because your enemy knows you are wise to past tactics. Nevertheless, the only choice you have is to either "Face Your Goliath", stay stuck on a new plateau, or most likely, go down in defeat.

While challenges are inevitable, "Goliaths" are more often than not of our own making. We often conquer one only to succumb to another.

Some examples:

- The addict who conquers alcoholism and then succumbs to drug addiction.
- The person, who hates their job, quits and moves to another, only to dislike that one too.
- The man who goes bankrupt and then promptly gets right back into overwhelming debt.
- The individual who quits shopping continuously and then begins to eat large quantities non-stop.
- The teen that overcomes an eating disorder and then turns to looking for love in all the wrong places.
- The man who completes anger management courses and then moves into compulsive exercise.
- The Dad who quits traveling too much to be home and then spends all his time at home on the Internet.
- The workaholic who realizes it and turns to

religious fanaticism as an antidote.
• The supreme manipulator, or "control freak" who
  tries to arrange the show, only to have people rebel
  and discount them.

Why does this phenomenon occur? Why do we, like David, find ourselves faced over and over again with a repetitious pattern of "Goliaths"?

Is it possible that we are confusing symptoms with root causes? In each of the above scenarios, the presenting face of Goliath is different. However, the common denominator is the individual involved. Wherever we go, there we are. David was the common factor both in victory over Goliath and downfall with Bathsheba. We are the common denominator in our own lives.

Remember, we began with the idea that we are powerless, in and of ourselves, to sustain needed change. One of the objectives of this book is to help you clearly identify repetitive patterns; to get down to root causes and conditions, and lay a foundation for a different manner of living.

It is a reality that most of our "Goliaths" are self imposed. When we change the way we think, and make different decisions, the number of "Goliaths" we face will drop drastically. The solution to our difficulties lies in changing what is inside, which produces fruit on our outside.

That is not to say that all situations that occur are of our own making. Accidents and tragedies occur. Bad things happen to good people, and to bad people. This is a different circumstance than those where we actively participate in our own demise, as David did in this situation.

The fact is godly David succumbed. Even the prophet Samuel had sons who "did not walk in his ways… and would accept a bribe… and would pervert judgment". It is a clear message to us we must develop our relationship with God. We must make this the primary focus of our efforts, as it is only there any continuing power to avoid "Resurgent Goliaths" is available.

Vigilance requires us to become resolute in serving God. Why? In this world, a victory over one strong enemy virtually assures challenges from other foes in different forms.

In victory, the potential to positively influence greater numbers grows, as does the potential to create greater havoc. You may have heard it this way: "To whom much is given, much is required." When we have been given a gift through victory over "Goliath", we dare not squander it by allowing ourselves the luxury of thinking we have "got it all figured out". We do not.

We have been given a design for our life that will work if we continue to use it. It will only work when it is in daily, moment to moment use and application. Set down the tools; unplug from the power, and watch destruction rush in.

We choose: Life in all its fullness, or destruction. The opposing armies are always there. We must continually be willing to pick up the "5 smooth stones, take our sling, and start across the valley to meet "Goliath." If we do our part, God will do His.

Stones for your sling:
Humility, staying right sized before God will pay big dividends. "Only the person who has conquered himself (by surrendering to God) can conquer his Goliaths."

[16]

The Portal of Surrender: Brokenness

When Nathan confronted David about his behavior and choices regarding Bathsheba, David entered a period of intense self-evaluation. He was a broken and contrite man. By broken, we mean he came to a place where he was acutely, painfully, devastatingly aware of the vast gap between what he knew to be right and the reality of his actions and thoughts. He could no longer deny the fact of his failure, sin, and the consequences. He had a "blinding flash of the obvious" that shattered his careful construct of denial and deception. It was then, he created the 51 Psalm. A key verse Palm 51:17 says: "The sacrifices to God are a broken spirit, A heart broken and crushed, O God, you will not despise."

He came to the point of realization; his greatest transgression was against God. He experienced the grieving of the spirit which comes when we realize we have devastated the most important, vital, and life giving relationship we know. It is the sort of grief that feels like your heart is torn into little pieces and can never be made whole again. It is debilitating in its intensity and conviction of the error of our ways is inescapable.

Condemnation, an exaggerated sense of our wrongness and a symptom of our self centered focus, is an experience of false remorse and self pity we can wallow in. Conviction, on the other hand, focuses on the principles we have violated and the accompanying consequences. It is focused outward toward God and others. It is always a harbinger of a deeper humility for us and a more accurate sense of who we really are.

Other verses of the 51st Psalm emphasize further principles on the matter of brokenness and our relationship with God. They are a cry from David's heart to God.
Brokenness was the catalyst to catapult him forward toward greater humility, understanding the need for mercy, dependence on God and His grace, and compassion for others. It drove his roots deeper into the soil of God's love,

Each of us will have our own times of brokenness. The question is: Will it make us move toward God, or away from Him?

As we have moved through this consideration of David's encounter with Goliath and events after there is a definite process that has emerged. Let's lay it out and look at what it has to do with brokenness and how we may grow through our own times "On the Potters Wheel".

Let's go back to the beginning and walk through what we have covered.

---

1. **The Samuel Principle**: We need Godly individuals to mentor and guide us. We need to remain teachable under their care.

2. **Morbid Fear**: Fear lies to us and keeps us frozen in place.

3. **Denial**: Denial lets us pretend what is real is not real. Eventually, our denial construct collapses and we are forced to deal with the fact that we do not have

the needed power to confront Goliath on our own. Because we lack power, our lives are inherently unmanageable.

4. **Powerlessness:** Our best thinking and unaided will are insufficient. We realize we must access power from God, as He is the only source with sufficiency to meet our need.

5. **Plugging In**: We determined that we need to ask God to come into our lives; to turn ourselves over into His care and control.

6. **Orienting Spiritually**: We examined the "Courage Compass" to learn how to properly orient to the Power source and how to let that power flow into and through us.

7. **Self Examination**: We examined ourselves to see what impediments are in our character impeding the flow of power. We asked God to remove those things and place His character into us.

8. **Straightening Out**: We determined to live a life of forgiveness and went about setting matters straight with those we have harmed.

9. **A New Center**: We now have a "New Center" that our life is to revolve around.

10. **Growing**: There is to be a continual process of growing into a larger and more effective spiritual state.

11. **Serving:** We are to give as freely as we have received; to be of maximum service to God and those about us.

12. **Resurgent Goliaths**: We are subject to relapsing into prideful self assurance if we forget that it is about God and not about us.

The key ingredient to successful consummation of the process outlined in these principles is humility, the willingness to surrender our will to the direction and control of God.

However, for most of us our self-will (our self oriented thinking and choices) is a powerful presence, and is not likely to go quietly. Many would persuasively argue that self is the thing we need to build up and protect. Notice in the previous paragraph, we stated that it is our will, the power of choice that is at issue, not the sense of self.

The reason is this: We seek to be the master of our will, determining what is right and wrong, true and false. We thus usurp the rightful place that God occupies; that of determining truth and what is right. As individuals, we make poor gods; better to let God Captain our ship as we have already shipwrecked ourselves in ways mild and profound.

Return for a moment to the proposition of powerlessness. If, as demonstrated, we do not even have the power to make things turn out as we desire on a consistent basis what makes us think we have the power to determine truth? Truth, by its very nature, cannot change and therefore cannot be altered to fit our whims or desires. This is what makes the direction of our will crucial.

What is subject to change is our individual grasp and understanding of truth. While we will never achieve a perfect understanding, we strive to become better and more effective students of God's truth. With that as our objective, the decision to submit our will, our power of choice, to God is a responsible and reasonable one.

Because there is a part of our self that seeks to protect itself at all costs it seeks that same "god" position for itself. Consequently, it is likely that we will encounter all manner of internal battles. When we allow this resurgence of self reliance to occur, we are headed to a certain appointment with failure. We are also deploying the forces that will turn like a boomerang and damage us. At those moments, we will come, as David did, face to face with the painful reality of the destruction we have wrought; that what is broken cannot be reassembled. The net result is experiencing brokenness ourselves, even as David did.

At these moments, we are squarely confronted with a choice. We face either move toward God, or move farther into our self. The brokenness we experience will either serve to take us deeper into our relationship with God, or to reinforce the notion that we can somehow win through on our own. What determines which road we take is our decision to surrender to God.

Should we choose the path of self, we are setting out to prove that our own power is sufficient to overcome any obstacle. What is absurd is this is the very effort that got us into this place already. If it were not so tragic, it would be laughable. In an effort to alleviate our pain, we often take this route, thinking it to be a way to immediately alleviate our suffering. The usual result is a return, in fairly short order, to an even more intense set of painful circumstances.

The other alternative is to surrender and face God, as David did. We can agree with Him; we have erred in ways that have created damage to others and ourselves. We can again examine ourselves in light of His truth, speak to Him about it, receive mercy and grace, and seek to let God plant and develop more of His character and ways into us. We lay down, again, the idea that we can do things by our own thought and power. We can see our brokenness for what it is, a symptom of the powerlessness and the unmanageability of our lives using our own meager resources.

Brokenness then, leads us to the place of surrender. We admit God is right. Our self-will is shaved of another portion of its independence of spirit (pride) in favor of the character of God being built into our thoughts and actions.

Surrender then, is not a stinging defeat. There is no down side. We choose to go with God rather than delay the inevitable and inflict more unnecessary pain on ourselves and others.
We say to God; "Use me for the purpose you made me for." We learn and develop a deepening humility before God; more of Him and less of us. As counter intuitive as it seems, we surrender to move ahead.

What is most marvelous is the experience of life in its absolute fullness, joy in abundance, and purposefulness that is certain.

Confusion will melt away. There may be occasional uncertainty but doubt will have no home in our soul. We will learn honesty before men and God. Fear of people will melt away. Gradually, we will come to depend on the inspiration of God in our moment to moment activity.

As we look back, we will see the hand of God in the outworking of situations and circumstances. When we face the present, having this reservoir of experience, we will find a growing and expanding trust in His direction. As we look toward the future, we will have faith and hope because we know who God is and what he does. That is a summary of David facing Goliath. It will be our story as well.

If you would like to learn more about specific activities and processes to integrate this series of principles into your life and character, we have developed some resources. Go to roar@ recoveryandredemptionpub.com for more information about how you can access them.

Stones for your sling:

Surrender is the key that unlocks the door. Brokenness is often the admission price. Both will pay handsome dividends if we will stay engaged.

[17]

Greg's Samuel's and David's: The Rest of the Story

In every life there are times when we encounter a "Goliath"; some thing, situation, circumstance, or person that appears unconquerable. Here is how this worked out in my story:

Alcoholism was only a symptom of extreme self-centeredness, self seeking, selfishness; this is my true "Goliath", my mortal enemy even though I thought it was my salvation for a long time. This "Goliath" masqueraded through various symptoms and activities over time. Ultimately, this "Goliath" promised me salvation and protection but delivered only destruction and death.

I have lived for six decades. You read about the first two decades as I came to physical maturity, went to school, and came to think I knew more than everyone. I was smarter and "unique"; the rules didn't apply to me!

As you saw, the second two decades were spent building and destroying a family and career. Self-centeredness took me into the depths of alcoholism, drug use, sexual lasciviousness, and ultimate destruction of everything that ought to have been dear, but was not. At the conclusion of the fourth decade, all of that activity led to a collision with the first of the "Goliaths" - alcoholism.

Into this morass of self pity and self absorption God sent a Samuel; call him "Mr. D". Mr. D was in his late 50's at the time, now 20 years ago. Mr. D was a man of faith, overtly and powerfully so. No flash, no sizzle in a societal sense; simply a quiet coffee business owner. He conducted a "Bible Study" in his office on Wednesday afternoons. A friend, sensing my desperation, invited me to attend. I had walked away from God decades earlier and had said I would never return.

My best thinking and choices had brought me to this point of utter despair and hopelessness. What I was doing was not working out very well. The thought flashed "What have you got to lose except misery and hopelessness?"

The group welcomed me unreservedly; an unexpected turn of events, as at this point in life no one was asking me to come back. Generally they were saying: Don't ever come back here!

Mr. D listened to my self pity rant and simply said; "Have you come to know God?" I was flabbergasted! What did that have to do with anything? I asked what he meant and he inquired if I had a personal relationship with God; had I asked him to come into my life and take control? I had never heard it put that way. I said: "No, I have not and do not intend to!"

He simply said: "It is apparent to me that you lack power to make the needed change in your life. God is a source of power that can bring about the needed change. Sooner or later, you will have to address this fact: Your life is a mess and you need help. The help you need has to come from a source outside yourself. All you have to do is ask." Stunned and humbled is the only way to describe the response that I experienced.

A few weeks later, and after further deep emotional and spiritual beatings, that simple conversation led to my asking God into my life in the lobby of the restaurant. I was forever altered. Thus commenced a long period of restoration, step by painful step. "Mr. D" was a "Samuel."

Two years later, following a move across country for another job, I encountered a man we'll call "TK". As I struggled to effectively fulfill the responsibilities of the new position, and cope with a divorce, he came along side. Although he was my subordinate in age and in the organization, he was my superior in maturity. He coached, counseled, listened, and confronted.

When the job ended in my termination, he simply invited me to a prayer retreat. In the late fall of the previous year, Dianna had confronted me about alcoholism. I had not dealt with the issue. In desperation, I went to the retreat and had a deep encounter with God. I really admitted for the first time my alcoholism and powerlessness in the presenting face of my "Goliath". "TK" was a "Samuel."

A position opened up in another state. Being sober, I married Dianna, moved across 3 states, and took on new responsibilities. There I encountered "Mac". "Mac" was older and wiser; what a gift! For two years, he mentored me, was patient and merciful, yet he held me accountable. When it came time to retire, he arranged for me to take his place in the business as the leader. "Mac" was a "Samuel".

After two years, the business contract was terminated. Once again, desperation was knocking at the door. My younger son left home at 161/2 years old, never to return. We moved to another town, started a business, lost $40,000 in 6 months and were flat broke. A position opened up 4 states away. Believing there was no choice, we moved, leaving behind a daughter in college and a son in High School. While sobriety was maintained, serenity was fleeting.

Upon arriving, a man named "JR" appeared. He was sober for 20 years and as steady as a rock. His wife was dying of cancer, yet he was able to minister to the needs of others and maintain calm and serenity. He taught me principles and how to rest peacefully in trying circumstances. When my Father passed unexpectedly, and 6 months later my Mother, he was there with words of comfort and strength. "JR" was a "Samuel".

That position ended when, after accomplishing all the goals set before me for a two year period in about 14 months, I was offered a pay reduction of $10,000 per year. A move back to my home state followed. I bought another business with proceeds from my parent's estate, operated it for two years and sold it for pennies on the dollar.

In the process, I encountered "BW". He offered me a position with his company. For the next several years, he trained, coached, mentored, and helped me rebuild my life. All he ever asked was that I work a fair day for the pay. "BW" was a "Samuel".

During this time, my personal, interior life was growing increasingly chaotic. Then, I asked "LJ" to help me. LJ was slightly younger than I, and had less sobriety time, but was more teachable than I and had learned lessons I had not. He taught me what he knew. He was a "Believer in God" as well as sober. My life was radically transformed from that day on. "LJ" was a "Samuel".

"LJ" sent me to be of service to others; to volunteer my time in a worthy cause. In the course of this, my wife and I began a Bible Study for recovering people; that led to a Recovery Ministry at the church we were attending; that led to an association with a national ministry; that led to serving as volunteer state representative for the organization; that led to helping others start groups; that led to being on staff at a multi-cultural (50% African American 20% Hispanic, 30% White) mega-church in a large city in the state; that led to developing a life change curriculum that directly touched the lives of over 700 people in 2 ½ years. We had become "Samuels".

Our time at that church ended when we were part of a reduction in staff. This turn of events ushered in a deeply painful period of searching and seeking direction, not to mention endeavoring to find gainful employment; at age 60, no easy task! During this period, three different individuals, with no prompting from me, said "You should write a book." I wrote it off as a "pipe dream".

Once again, God sent a "Samuel".

After some months an opportunity to participate in a sales training course arose. We made a decision that I would enroll. The schedule was Monday to Friday, 7 to 4. I had to make 120 to 160 cold calls per day; it was brutal. During the 3rd week, on a Thursday afternoon at about 3:30 I experienced an overwhelmingly strong urge to depart.

I sensed there was a meeting to attend with someone. What was strange was that I had no meeting scheduled with anyone. It was as if an invisible hand was shoving me out the door. Having learned that spiritual forces move in unfamiliar ways, I left, not knowing where I was going or whom I was to "meet".

I walked to the Light Rail Station near the office where I was, validated my ticket and prepared to board. Generally, I rode toward the back of the train. This day, I sensed I was to board at the very front. The train came. I boarded, sat down, and pulled out a book I was reading by Bishop Daryl Brister titled "Doing Right in a Wrong World".

Two stops later a grey headed African American gentleman boarded and sat across from me. (I am as white as can be.) It was a fall day and the wind was blowing. He shivered a bit as he sat down. People on the train generally do not talk to one another. I-Pods are the order of the day – isolate and do not interact is the unspoken rule. I smiled at him and said: "It's a little breezy today isn't it?" He smiled back and said "Yes it is!"

We began to chat, asking about kids and grandkids, the weather, the usual fare. We agreed that children and grandchildren are incredible gifts. During the ensuing conversation, I inquired as to what he did for a living. He said "I do a number of things. Right now, I am a writer." We chatted about the type of books he wrote, and he indicated that he co-wrote some books and was currently involved in a project.

Being a gentleman, he asked what I did. I mentioned that until recently, I was a pastor at a local church. He asked which one, and I told him. He said, "I know of that Church. People from that church used to come into a restaurant I owned and eat." He listened intently as I described the work we had been doing. We talked all the way to the end of the line where we both had to get off.

As we were leaving, he asked for a Business Card so he could keep in touch. I did not have one, so I pulled out a copy of my Resume and handed it to him, indicating that it had my contact information on it. He looked directly into my eyes and said: "You should write a book! Would you spend a few more minutes with me?" I was shaken to my core, and intrigued at the same time. I agreed to meet him at a local restaurant a few blocks away.

By the time I arrived, he had read my resume and sat down with me. He proceeded to "read my mail" about who I was and what my characteristics were. To say I was dumbfounded is an understatement. He topped it off by saying: "I have a topic for your book. I will, within 48 hours, send you an outline and a purpose statement." Disbelieving, I agreed. I left thinking: "Either this man is the best con man I have encountered, or he is for real. There is no middle ground here."

Another "Samuel", the most potent one yet, had been sent my direction. The very next morning, Friday, at 10:00 am, as I was making my daily round of prospecting phone calls, my cell phone rang. My newest "Samuel" was on the line asking if I had checked my e-mail. As I had not, I told him that I would review it when I got home and reply via e-mail.

When I arrived home, I found the promised book topic and purpose statement in my in-box. It was well thought out, insightful, and thorough. Disconcerted, my review was cursory. However, a few suggestions and additions were noted and I hit the reply button thinking I was unlikely to hear anymore.

My heart was jaded and broken, and it showed. I did not believe people really helped one another any more. People can claim to be Samuels and turn out to be wolves in sheep's clothing instead.

Saturday morning, my phone rang once again; it was "Samuel". He asked if I would meet him to talk about the book. I hesitantly agreed. Thus commenced what has become one of the most treasured friendships of my life. This man unreservedly loved a stranger in the way only a "Good Samaritan's heart" can. He has continued to pick me up, dust me off, coach, counsel, confront, and pour blessings into my life. He was "Hope with skin on!"

In the eyes of the world, we are an unlikely pair: Black and white, different culturally and experientially. He is a PHD, stockbroker, businessman, entrepreneur, and published author. I was a broken pastor, sober alcoholic, financially strapped, bereft of hope individual. Yet God, in his mercy and wisdom, sent him to lift me up. All I had to do was be humble enough to be willing to receive from a man who was willing; a man on "Gods errand!" Samuel to my "David need."

"Samuel" later told me that on that Thursday afternoon, he was in a meeting and suddenly felt a strong urge to leave to meet someone. As he had been invited to the grand opening of a local celebrity's business, he went there thinking perhaps he was supposed to meet someone there. After a few minutes, he realized that he was to be somewhere else. He still was unsure of who he was supposed to meet.

He proceeded to the light rail stop. He usually sat to the rear of the train, but this day it seemed he was to get on the front of the train. He sat down across from me.

God sends "Samuels" to every "David". He can send them because they are listening to Him. They respond to His voice and go to where he directs them even if it makes no "sense." They trust their God!

He has sent them to you before, and when you are willing, will send another at the precise point of your need. "Samuel" will show up, do his work, and witness your "Davidic victory". Then, God will send you, if you listen and are willing, to be a "Samuel" to another "David" who "Faces Their Own Goliath".

Stones for your sling:

In every life there are times when we encounter a "Goliath"; some thing, situation, circumstance, or person that appears unconquerable. Extreme self-centeredness, self seeking, selfishness; this was my "Goliath", my mortal enemy even though I thought it was my salvation for a long time.

God sends "Samuels" to every "David". He can send them because they are listening to Him. They respond to His voice and go to where he directs them even if it makes no "sense." They trust their God!

When you are willing, He will send another at the precise point of your need.

Then God will send you, if you listen and are willing, to be a "Samuel" to another "David."

[18]

Dianna's Samuel's and David's: The Rest of the Story

I want to tell about our love story with God and with each other.

While I was in the treatment program, we were encouraged to find someone to mentor us. In some of the meetings, I met a woman I'll call "MC". She was 7 years sober and a gentle soul. I didn't know I could live a different way and be okay. Being sober meant a complete 180 degree change in the way I approached my life. MC was serene and peaceful in her approach to life.

She spent time with me taking walks, meeting me in my home with my three children, helping me with my step-work, listening to me and overall quietly loving on me. I had hope for the very first time in my life. I was 33 years old and knew I was going to be okay and that my life would be more than I could ever expect. MC was a Samuel who loved me and my family unreservedly. She continues to do so to this day.

Greg and I married July 8, 1989, in Dubuque and moved to Colorado later that month. As I look back I am very grateful for the recovery program as it has kept our marriage together. We were both relatively new to sobriety and had custody of all five of our children; his two sons and my three; a daughter and two sons, all five between the ages of 10-14.

Moving to the Colorado Mountains 20 miles northwest of Winter Park triggered old pain from childhood in Alaska. I began to look at the fact that I had been sexually abused as a child. It took me being two years sober for that to come up. God knew I was ready to deal with it. I wasn't feeling so ready; however, I had his guidance through the recovery.

My husband was really thrown for a loop. Before we married, he had asked me if I was ever sexually abused, and I had said no. At the time, those memories were deeply buried. He had experience in his previous relationship with this, and had indicated that he did not desire to encounter that another time. He has told me it took all the willingness he had to stay and try to work through it with me. Only God's grace is sufficient!

There was quite a bit of stress from the move, blending a family, teenagers, early recovery, newly married, new jobs, and more. I experienced a lot of rage. Uncontrollable outbursts! During this time, I was diagnosed with Post Traumatic Stress Disorder (PTSD) and then Bi-polar disorder in succession. The therapists were mystified by my symptoms. They tried everything they knew, to little positive effect. Our home life was often chaotic for everyone.

I continued with my attendance at recovery meetings and found a new sponsor. This work in my program is what kept my life and marriage together. I will always be eternally grateful that my husband has also been on this path—we have a common language and common solutions!!

We moved to Wisconsin in November of 1994 after a few brutal years in Colorado. There I met my new Samuel: "SS". She had 18 years of sobriety at the time and I thought she was lying. I could not imagine that someone could be sober that long and be happy about it—and she was. She was a determined and firm sponsor who worked the steps and expected me to do as she directed. I did!!

She asked me what recovery step I thought I was on? I said "Oh, probably, step 10 or 11". She said "I don't think you HAVE EVER DONE THE 2ND PART OF STEP 1. You don't believe your life is unmanageable."

I was insulted and wanted to smack her in the face.

However, when I went home and thought about it I realized she was absolutely right. Those words over time would save my life.

I had been controlling everything and doing it my way, I had not taken a drink or a drug, however, I was a dry drunk—no alcohol, yet angry and controlling. So I say to you when you are working with God on your recovery remember, there are two parts to begin with: powerlessness and unmanageability.

I had to come to believe that a power greater than me could restore me to sanity.

The power has to come from above! This is the only way for me to have any sanity in my life. My mind plays tricks on me. I have spent many years in recovery relying on my own power. It kept me resentful, angry, fear based, and really no fun to be around. If I could have, I would have gotten cleaned up by my own power.

In fact, because I treasure my intelligence it gets in the way of letting God have His way in my life. This has always reminded me that I have hit my bottom. For any good thing to happen with my life and for God to use me in the Kingdom, I must have help from a power source outside myself.

Oh my, I have battled this for years. I have put myself in the God chair so much I can't even begin to tell you how painful I have made my life. When I got cleaned up and made a decision to let God be in charge, it was a challenging process. Today, my life IS NO LONGER MY OWN.

I want you to really hear this. <u>Your life is not yours, my life is not mine.</u> For me to be happy and effective in the Kingdom of God my Life and my Will is turned over to Him daily. Sometimes I have to do this 20 times a day, because I relapse into control thinking, wanting what I want, when I want it and needing to be comfortable in my own skin all the time—that is clearly not letting God be in charge of my life. SS was a Samuel in my life.

We were in Wisconsin for only 17 months. When we returned to Grand Junction, Colorado, I met another Samuel: "Gigi". I asked for help to reorient my compass. What a woman of truth. She had wisdom beyond measure. I was still struggling with so much rage.

Through some additional testing I was diagnosed as having Borderline Personality Disorder. All I knew is I had a 'rage' issue. I was financially acting out with credit cards, near divorce, and couldn't imagine that I would have some rough days ahead. Why me? How could this be happening! I am nine years sober, worked the steps often and to the best of my ability—yet continued trading one addiction for another.

My husband later told me he was told that I would never recover from the narcissistic self absorption that is characteristic of this particular diagnosis. He told me that he told the therapist that he was vastly underestimating the power of God. He loved God, and so he loved me and stood by my side.

GiGi helped me deal with the day to day and have integrity with myself. Listening to her helped me to transfer these new skills into marriage, parenting, career, and ministry. Little by little I began to feel better. However, I eventually exhausted her ability to be of assistance. Gigi was a Samuel.

After a period of time I got to a place of desperation where the medications and strategies I was pursuing left me bereft of hope once again. I could not sleep, and fear of everything had me in its grip. I felt as if sanity was slipping away moment by moment. God directed me to a wise physician, a psychiatrist.

At long last, someone was able to get to the root of some of my medical and psychological issues. She was able to profoundly help me with a clear diagnosis of Dysthymic Disorder and medication to alleviate the symptoms. At long last, I began to stabilize in mood and temperament. What a blessing! Even though the doctor was not a Samuel, she certainly was a godsend in my life.

We had become involved in a local church. After several attempts to be part of some Bible studies, it was evident that as recovering individuals, we had some unique perspectives and needs. I had said to my husband—"the church we are going to does not have anything for addicts—let's start a group."

With the blessing of the pastor we started a bible study in our home. We promoted this study in the church bulletin for addicts and those affected by an addict. I couldn't believe it—15 people came to the first meeting. We studied out of the workbook "Experiencing God" and applied the principles to recovery issues.

In July of 2000, my youngest son married. I was participating in a Christian Women's group that met monthly. There was a special speaker from Fort Collins and husbands could join us for a Friday night Dinner/Speaker meeting. All I can remember is that he talked about God and asked if anyone in the room needed to give their heart and life to God.

I knew God was calling me—I quietly said the prayer to myself. When I returned home I told my husband. I knew my life was about to change dramatically. In August of 2000 I was baptized at Connected Lakes a State Park outside the city of Grand Junction. This encounter was another of the many Samuels that would enter my life.

Over the years in my recovery, I have been more teachable and willing to listen to feedback. I can tell you that talking about my sexual life was the hardest to share. Because I had been hurt so badly by multiple perpetrators I was uneasy about how it would all turn out.

However, as usual God showed up and I have received the most healing in this area. I am human with human emotions and responses and I participated in very unhealthy relationships all my life. I am grateful today that talking about sex is okay in recovery.

life. I am grateful today that talking about sex is okay in recovery. It is about freedom!!

Moving to Denver was a big promotion from God. After many years of walking out my recovery, God promoted me to a Pastor position at a large Church in Denver. Talk about being right smack in the middle of God's Will for my life. Greg and I started a recovery program. I was in my element!! Sober, healthy, and helping others in church. I walked side by side the many men and women God sent. I also was blessed to be on staff with amazing Men and Women of God who day by day spoke truth and encouragement into my life.

After three years in this position Greg and I were part of a staff downsizing, for reasons I still do not understand today; however, it has been some of the richest time in my Walk with the Lord.

Again, as usual God sent an amazing woman in recovery. Samuels seem to pop up everywhere as long as I am willing to acknowledge them. "Dee" has listened, encouraged and challenged me to continue to look at my part in life and to clean up the wreckage on a day to day basis. I have come to learn about being teachable on a whole new level. I call her daily. I talk about what is going on in my life. She is steady and hears me. I always come away from these conversations confronted with ugly character defects and the willingness to change. My desire is to be more like our Leader daily.

I still have struggles with emotional over-eating, low self-esteem, personally and emotionally taking on other people's stuff and selfishness.

Here is a list of root issues I have had the chance to look at and move toward healing from:

- Rage
- Selfishness
- Fear

- Sexual abuse
- Emotional abuse
- Physical abuse
- Sexual sin
- Abandonment
- Rejection
- Emotional neglect
- Physical neglect
- Overeating
- Overspending
- Smoking
- Emotionally shut down
- Resentment
- Financially irresponsible
- Self-loathing
- Laziness
- Swearing
- Impatience
- Demanding
- Rude
- Jealousy
- Arrogance

Through prayer and meditation I work to improve conscious interaction with God. I seek and pray for knowledge of His Will for me and power to do it.

This is simple and very straight forward; I seek God's will through my life DAILY through prayer, meditation and reading in His Word. I pray for His Will and the power to make it happen.

Because, I struggle with fear and lack the courage I seek Him for that, and guess what, when I ask, He provides and it works out every time. This is a moment to moment process on a daily basis.

I have had a spiritual experience as the result of this, so I endeavor to give away what I have received.

There is so much to say here. First of all, we will HAVE A SPIRITUAL EXPERIENCE. Do you realize what that means, it means your life will change; **it is a promise**. That is big!! I don't know about you but, I came with NO HOPE!! I felt the hope in the process and I knew there was something for me and I was going to do what I had to do to receive it.

I want to say my spiritual experiences came in all sorts of ways.

Some were so fast I could hardly absorb them; some came so slow I wondered if I could hang on one more minute. I can tell you that the work is worth it, the sacrifices are worth it, the change in lifestyle is so worth it.

Another part of this is **in helping others**. I would not be here if the people before me would have been selfish and chosen not to turn around and help someone after they received their healing. I can tell you that I have very little patience for people who receive healing and then just disappear.

So, I ask you, as you begin to receive your healing, please be praying to God about how and where He would have you serve, then do it. Not only will your life be blessed eternally, but here on earth, right now, you will receive the joy of watching others and helping them on their road to recovery.

In writing this, I have been reflecting that the greatness of God overwhelms me. There have been some tough spots, tough years in my life and yet God is right there walking me though each one.

Another example—the unemployment from last year was a tough time. I knew God had not changed His call on my life; however, the days did not make sense. My husband couldn't buy a job. Then another Samuel entered our lives—a true man of God; a jack of all trades when it comes to business and God. He is the reason this book evolved. The lessons have been tremendous and stretching. I have had to go deep into my relationship with Christ to walk out the days.

I am humbled to say that through the past 20 years of marriage with Greg I have never, ever loved this deeply. Not because I am anything great, but because God is great. I can say as a matter of fact that the godly principles outlined in this book have kept me married and in love like never before. There have been major ups and downs and yet always a willingness to do the next right thing. I look forward to many more years of learning to give and receive love.

DON'T QUIT BEFORE THE MIRACLE HAPPENS— YOU NEVER KNOW WHAT PARTS OF THE PROCESS ARE GOING TO HOLD YOUR MIRACLES!!

Stones for your sling:
Only God's grace is sufficient!
So I say to you when you are working with God on your recovery remember there are two parts to begin with: powerlessness and unmanageability.

DON'T QUIT BEFORE THE MIRACLE HAPPENS—YOU NEVER KNOW WHAT PARTS OF THE PROCESS ARE GOING TO HOLD YOUR MIRACLES!!

[19]

Life in the Discomfort Zone: Growing Better Not Bitter

As you read "The Rest of the Story" chapters, perhaps you noticed some patterns. The moving, a period of employment and relative stability, followed by an abrupt ending, initiating a period of seeking and searching, followed by another repetition of the pattern. One "Goliath Faced"; another waiting in the wings ready to spring forth on cue. The common denominator was the individuals involved; Dianna and I.

After we wrote the stories, I (Greg) was deeply troubled for a period. I was distressed at the patterns revealed. I began to despair, wondering if there had been any progress. I was once again forcefully confronted with my shortcomings and failures; Writing my actions and history down in black and white does that. I can no longer pretend what happened did not happen. I am confronted with reality. Brokenness was once again my companion.

Would I surrender? Would I take the opportunity to mine the experiences for all the lessons they hold; to grow better, not bitter. As I spoke with my "Samuel" about the shame and embarrassment I felt at what I had seen, he said this: "You need to write about what this has produced. You are asking the right question: What do I do now?"

So, I elected to surrender, to make a further examination. When I did, looking for Gods work in each situation, other patterns emerged for consideration:

- A continual, boundless measure of God's grace, mercy, kindness, and an outpouring of His love in our lives and the life of our family, and in those whose lives we influence.
- What began as a virulent form of co-dependency has been transformed by the power of God's love into mutual interdependence: a principled agape love for each other that transcends the Goliath difficulties we have faced individually and together.
- Romantic love grew in proportion to agape love, and deepens and blossoms as agape love is exercised. Love is following God's ways no matter what Goliath we encounter.
- Each change resulted in an expansion of perspective; sobriety was maintained intact. It was not situation dependant.
- A gradual move from exclusively secular positions to community service roles.
- A shift from "It's about me" to an "It's about others" thought process.
- A continuing presence of "Samuels" to provide spiritual guidance and mentoring.
- Development of an effective way to help and serve others.
- Opportunities to mentor others in their time of need as they "Face Their Own Goliath."
- A continual stream of difficult, painful transitions

and growth.

- Shedding of old roles and functions to move into new ones.
- When a season of time was up, for whatever reason, it came to an end. If I didn't move willingly, circumstances moved us forcefully.
- Each ending contained the seeds of a new beginning.
- There has been a sustained presence and recurrence of uncomfortable, often deeply painful challenges to our faith, sense of self, relationship with God, and with others.

Over a period of time, a complete metamorphosis has taken place. Individuals who were so self-absorbed that they could not see any way out of self imposed crises transitioned into pastoral roles mentoring hundreds.

From "serve me" to "serve you" the perspective shift continues in pursuit of developing a God oriented life.

Transformation is difficult and painful because it requires we lay down what we are familiar with, even if ineffective, and pick up what we are unfamiliar with and begin to use it. It always requires a sacrifice of some part of our selves in favor of a character attribute of God. It is a faith walk, trusting in God ever more profoundly.

This is evidenced as we exhibit:

- mercy instead of anger
- grace instead of retribution
- forgiveness instead of resentment
- honesty instead of lying
- integrity instead of self gratification
- courage instead of fear

- standing for principle instead of living for approval

The list is limited only by our willingness to stay engaged with God. Our pain is in direct proportion to our resistance to His work in and through us. We choose our attitude about our level of discomfort, but we cannot avoid discomfort. Pain is inevitable, but misery is optional. The path we are on mandates a continuing level of "life in the discomfort zone".

Growth, transformation, and strengthening will involve a level of personal pain and discomfort that we cannot control. We can only move through it, and we can only be defeated by unwillingness to pass through. That is the bad news.

The good news is that it is "pain with a purpose." The love of God is truly transforming. The Prophet Isaiah described the coming Messiah and his pain that was for a purpose (Isaiah Chapter 53). So too, our pain can be turned toward a purpose in God's economy. Instead of just suffering for no reason, we learn that we suffer for a purpose. The purpose is to draw us further into the character of God and to exhibit more of His character in us for the benefit of others. We will grow larger in our capacity for love, mercy, and grace as we go on.

This is not personal martyrdom. It is not to glorify our pain to draw attention to ourselves. It is about going quietly and humbly with God and trusting that as we do He will show us more of Himself and we will experience the joy of His presence. While this may seem esoteric, be assured that it is not. In fact, it is the most practical thing we can know.

Pleasure comes and goes, momentary and fleeting, and constant pursuit of it wears a person out. Pleasure is typically sensually rooted and connected to events and people. Pleasure demands more and more of it to produce the same effect. Pleasure can coexist with pain, yet is antithetical to it and seeks to obscure and /or mask it. Happiness and sadness are often connected in some measure as well. Pleasure and pain in this environment are impediments to our development as the focus is not on principle.

Joy is radically different. Joy comes from the love, presence, and glory of God and is a fruit of His Spirit (see Galatians Chapter 5). As we experience and learn of it, we find it simpler to attain; simple, but not easy. Great truth is generally simple. Do not confuse simplicity with ease of implementation. All that is required is simple obedience; doing the right thing because it is the right thing to do.

Joy can coexist with pain, and has within it the capacity to redirect the effect of pain as a force toward growth instead of an impediment. Pain becomes secondary and subservient to the fruit of Joy. Joy is independent of pain and supersedes it. Because Joy emanates from God, it is an unstoppable force. Once a person has got a hold of Joy, he will pay whatever price is necessary to maintain it.

There are many examples of this: David who faced Goliath and experienced the joy of standing for his God; The soldier who sacrifices time and perhaps is severely injured and yet talks of the joy of serving. There is the individual, like Mother Teresa who willingly wades into the worst of slums and speaks of her joy in doing so. There is the leader like Mandela who endures tremendous hardship and emerges victorious and joyful. The Bible tells of Jesus Christ who for the joy set before Him endured pain and death for everyone. What is evident is that joy is the symptom of selflessness in the service God.

- Each of these examples has these factors in common:
- Each experienced the love of God in their life. As a result:
- Each had Hope in their God that energized them to action.
- Each had Faith in their God that led them to courage.
- Each had Courage that led them to specific action.

[20]

Getting Connected:
Plugging into the Power

Well, here we are; Powerless, unmanageable, needing regeneration of body, mind, soul, and spirit. Having concluded all of this, recognizing something must change and we are powerless to do it on our own, a question forms, "Now what?"

Rather than "Now what?" a more appropriate query might be *"Now who?"*

"What," you may ask, "do you mean by that?"

"**Now who?**" puts the question in the proper framework. Power resides in a source, not a what, but who; God (Yahweh, Jehovah). He is the personage of the highest order, self sufficient, fully complete, all powerful. It cannot be otherwise or it would not be a power ultimately greater than our selves. All other known power sources are finite in nature, just as we are, and are therefore limited in their capacity.

What we are requiring to effect the needed change in us is a power source which is without limit, either in time, space, or purpose.

Any lesser Source is inviting the continuing disaster we are seeking to free our selves from.

So, "How do we plug in?" How do we connect with this Power Source? Does such a source exist at all?

You may be thinking: "I simply cannot make such a leap of faith; to believe in something I cannot touch, feel, or see." Really?

Let us ask some questions of ourselves:

- Do you go to bed at night anticipating waking up?
- Do you stop at red lights expecting others to do the same?
- Do you flip the light switch, thinking the lights will come on?
- Do you go to the store in the belief the shelves will be stocked?
- Do you express love, or hatred, expecting the message to be heard?
- Do you eat believing the food will nourish your body?

Isn't each of these a simple act of faith? Isn't it true that each of these simple beliefs is based on a track record of experience, known either personally or collectively by society? In other words, there is credibility to them based on personal involvement. There is really no "leap" to it.

Can you see electricity? Have you seen love? No, you have not. You have observed the effect of electricity. You have seen acts of love. The verifiable source of these things is intangible, yet we know they are real. None of us denies that love exists.

When considering the reality of God, we are trapped by the fact that there exists no physical person or anything with "skin on" that we can see or touch. Simple logic states that every house is built by someone. The Bible offers God as the Creator of all things, the builder of the house. Anything with design or purpose must have a Creator.

The Scriptures report that everything God has said He will do, He has done. The report is there for us to accept. There is no more trustworthy Personage than He. His record is perfect... Check it out for yourself.

There exists a greater body of testimony to God's faithfulness than for any other thing, person, or fact that we know of. There is no real need to make blind steps any more than there is a need to wonder if electricity works. David's faith in God's power was rewarded.

Faith is a normal part of our existence. In fact, if you stop and think, almost everything we do is based in faith. The most reasonable posture of a person is that of faith. So, our ability to exercise faith is not in question. The question is not can I or do I believe; it is what do I believe?

Another point to consider is this: there is a difference between faith and credibility (being credible or believable). As we have seen, faith is based on a history of trustworthiness; of consistent performance.

Credibility only has to meet the test of seeming plausible, somewhat believable, without the basis of past performance. Something can seem credible without actually being true or doing what is promised. If something is incredible, it does not even meet the believability test. The suggestion is that a good deal of our thinking may have been credible, but did not produce fruit. Some of our thinking may have met the incredible test; not believable at all.

In light of this, faith seems a much saner basis for living. Consider:

Was not each of us abjectly faithful to the failed belief systems that brought us to the brink of total collapse that we have sought to remedy? Did we not remain loyal to the thinking that kept us believing in the power of our "Goliath"?

Here is another point to ponder: Power is relational in nature.

One must be connected to it to access and use it. The flow of power moves from the source, giving life and purpose to that which is connected to it. Those connected to it in turn produce benefit to those around them.

Consider the example of the fire which cooks food, or the light bulb that brightens a room. Witness the water faucet that must be connected to the well and offers the quenching drink to the thirsty. Look at the tree that must be planted in the earth and gives shade and lumber for building. Experience the love that must flow from a pure heart and that nourishes the recipient's soul; the tears that must be shed from a compassionate eye that convey caring and understanding.

None could function apart from their wellspring, their power source.

Consider also the frauds, the look-alikes, the empty wells: The windmill promising a drink which turns out to be connected to a dry hole; the tree appearing alive but already dead because its roots have withered. Remember the Lover who promised to endure but really used us for their own feeble purposes and walked away. Recall the tears that were shed for effect but ceased as soon as the intended result was achieved.

Each of these has no power connection at all except to their self serving desires. All seek only to disconnect us, to leave us ever more powerless and distraught. Of relationship, there is only a shadow to create the illusion of care that distracts us from the reality of the life destroying and deadly aim inherent in them.

Does a dog pray before it eats the Dog Chow? No!

It simply consumes what is set in front of it with no thought of the consequence to the food source. Nevertheless, it instinctually wags its tail as if approving its master's gift.

Think of it this way: There is a difference between a "Preying

Mantis" and a "Praying Man". While both imitate the posture of prayer, one is seeking to grab and kill prey, while the other is praying and seeking power to be useful.

Ultimately, we have to connect to the source of power to overcome the powerless state we are in. We must enter into relationship with this power, this whom that God is. For so many of us, that is embodied in the model set in the Greek Scriptures by Jesus Christ.

Perhaps you are weary and are seeking relief.

As God is the power source, we must, in our brokenness rely on Him. Mercy may be defined as kindness beyond what justice requires. It flows when we don't receive that penalty we are justly due, and grace is being given that which we don't deserve. We begin to understand our desperate need for power to overcome.

We begin to learn to seek and follow a greater power than ourselves. Power begins to move in and through us.

We begin to experience peace of mind; A Spirit of mildness begins to take root in us. We sense that we have been somehow washed clean, redeemed in a wonderful, unfathomable way.

We begin to really comprehend that there is truly only one ultimate power source. We become willing to be "called out" of our broken life:

Our senses become heightened by a spiritual renewal within us that we cannot adequately describe. Quietness of spirit and mind become treasures of our hope for a new life and evidence at once of its arrival.

We find that our position in life has changed. We are plugged into things that we had hardly dared dream of before and now they are realities in our life. In the end, we find that we have tapped into an infinite source of power; like an ocean of pure, life giving water that surges to, up into, and through us in a mighty flood. Yet it is so gentle that we are not overcome but rather lifted up.

Have you made the decision? Have you invited God to come

into your life? If not, and you have decided to do so, pray a prayer and ask the true God to come in, forgive, renew, and transform you by His spirit.

Maybe you have asked Him to be your God, but haven't turned some of your will over to Him. You have invited God into the entry way, but have kept Him standing there. You have reserved some "Closet" space, some arena in your life that you are hanging onto. Maybe that is the area that is causing you the greatest difficulty now? That is your "Goliath".

If that is you, I urge you to go to Him in prayer and totally surrender yourself and that area, those decisions and choices to Him, NOW!

He is God, or He is not; what is your choice to be?

We simply need to ask to enter into relationship. We simply make a decision to turn all of our life; all that we say, think, and do over to the care and control of God. Nothing more needs to be said.

[21]

Face Your Own Goliath: Faith, Hope and Courage

Whether you are currently Facing Your Own Goliath, or have successfully challenged Goliath already, it is essential you clearly understand and access your power source on a continuous basis.

David encountered success because he was "plugged into the power." REMEMBER: Power is relational. He had hope because he knew who his God was, and understood that his God was more powerful than any situation he faced or would face. He had faith and lived it out.

His faith was based in the track record of his God. God had proven him self trustworthy in the past. In every encounter David had with the bear and lion, God had come through. David's faith was based in real, tangible experience. Though God was invisible, his presence and action were tangibly evident as David went about the work assigned to him. He stayed in a relationship with his God.

He could exhibit selflessness and courage because he had faith and hope. The outcome was not dependent on David; it was dependant on his God and God's power flowing to and through him. He could serve in a maximum degree because his power source came from outside himself. Selfishness is a personal issue; selflessness is a God issue. Fear is a personal issue; courage is a God issue.

David's love for God was the wellspring of his activities. God's love for David was the source of his power. God's Spirit with David was the wisdom and skill evidenced in the victory over Goliath.

It was not David's strength that carried the day. It was his certainty in the might, power, and sovereignty of his God that mattered. David succeeded because he had faith. He took God at His word and acted accordingly. He was devoid of pretense.

He maintained a reverential fear of God; he did not let mortal fear of man, or morbid fear of man, override his reverence for God and determination to follow Him. Thus his path was made straight, his actions clear, the aim sure, the enemy powerless, the victory complete, the influence wide, the consequences far reaching, and the message delivered through the ages.

David's battle with Goliath has inspired every person who has heard the story. What is it that is at work? You may remember that we said this: "God inspired and spirit empowered action have an effect unlike any other activity. Because God is at work, His spirit is uniquely attractive and instructive at the same time. People are drawn in and lifted up and they often don't know why. But they will generally be led to inquire about the experience. Real truth does that!"

Consider the following:

- Perhaps you have had the experience of feeling trapped by circumstances and seeing no way out. Have you experienced despair that "things" will never get better? Have you ever wondered if you would ever really change? Have you watched your life spiral out of control, go from bad to worse, with a "hurricane" swamping your boat?

- Has gut wrenching pain wracked your mind, body, or both to the point that you think you can't take it anymore? Have you ever just run away and hid, trying anything to evade something you just couldn't deal with?

- Have loved ones betrayed you? Has someone you trusted stabbed you in the back? Have you been manipulated or taken advantage of? Were you abused and suffered grave physical and emotional damage?

Any of these situations can become a "Goliath" lurking around in our lives. It can be obvious, shouting its presence every moment, tormenting us incessantly. Or, maybe we bury "Goliath" deep in the recesses of our mind and heart like a tumor waiting to explode. Perhaps it becomes a "Plain Secret", sitting in plain sight right in the middle of the living room of our life but no one talks about it.

Whatever the case, remember the course of spiritual action to "Face Your Own Goliath", just as David did. God inspired action is yours for the asking. God is timeless and eternal. He does not change; He is the same yesterday, today, and forever. What he did for David, He will do for us.

Hope is not an "I sort of, maybe, possibly" abstract possibility. Hope is the certainty of God's presence in and through you when you engage with Him and surrender yourself to Him.

Thus will you walk in faith as you; having received God, listen to your "Samuels", orient to spiritual north, pick up "5 smooth stones". Courage will evidence as you engage "Goliath", deliver a death blow to that enemy, walk in victory, and influence the Army to go forth.

No matter how many "Goliaths" appear before you, God is God of all. Will he remain your God?

[22]

Roar! Our God Given Voice

When we began this journey, Goliath was roaring his challenge at us with all the venom and menace possible. Real and imagined threats abounded. Terror had been our constant companion. We sought solace wherever we could. Hopelessness and a sense of powerless victim-hood seemed to be our destiny.

We could hardly speak about our circumstances in a rational manner much less have any sense of a course of action. Victory over Goliath appeared impossible. Confronting Goliath certainly seemed like asking to be decimated in every way possible. Like the Israelite Army when David arrived, we listened to the taunts and cowered in fear. Dimly aware that victory was possible, we really believed it implausible. Our previous defeats certainly had us convinced that it was useless to resist.

Whatever our personal journeys and presenting symptoms, our common experience was of often repeated, bone jarring, spirit crushing demoralization and defeat. No weapon we could muster proved sufficient to sustain long term victory. While we encountered some success, perhaps even spectacularly so, it was inevitably followed by still greater setbacks. Ultimately, we came to a place of realization that Goliath seemed invincible. Our only course seemed to be to plod on to the bitter end – whatever that might be.

We now realize that our previous state was not reality at all. We have traveled the path to Facing Our Own Goliath and have successfully embarked on the journey. We have connected with God in a profound manner and have tapped a power that has sparked revolutionary changes in us, our thinking, and our actions.

We have a solid basis for faith and effective tactics for action. Our new reality is one of sound thinking based in the truth of God. We no longer cower in fear before the voice and taunts of Goliath. In fact, we have a new found voice of our own – the voice of faith.

We, like David, have a solid basis for speaking in confidence and boldness because we have lived it as David did. The existence and power of God is no longer a theory, an illusory concept, a nice story, or some hoped for occurrence. It has become fact for us. It is certainty beyond certainty; it is a knowing that we know that we know.

Having been moved by the power of God from fear to faith, from inaction to action, from hopelessness to courage there is a peace and calm that surpasses any thing we could have ever done on our own.

The question is not if we will Face Our Own Goliath, the question is when. We know the how: in the power and strength of God.

Thus fortified, the wonder of David's words possess a fresh, vibrant clarity that is now a clear call for us to find our own God given voice and words.

We have come to understand that when empowered and led by God, the words of our mouth are powerful beyond measure, even as they were for David.

David's words of faith were not those of a man speaking "Positive Affirmations" or some "Secret". He was not a man who believed that he could attract whatever he wanted into his life by simply saying it was so. He knew better. We must humble ourselves and rely on the true God! Those words are simple to say and with His help, simple to fulfill.

Dianna and I have learned that lesson.

God has brought us victory, and will bring victory to you as one of His People. Our words are to mirror the qualities and character of the true God as He gives us voice. We are to ROAR! Not as Goliath did, boasting about ourselves, but as David did: shouting the praises of God and declaring His magnificent qualities.

Face Your Own Goliath is our ROAR!

What will be your ROAR!?

Now, it is time to cross the valley, running!

The victory is already won, only your faith is necessary.

Walk with God, BE Fearless!

Conquer today's Goliath and Roar!

Please, Be Blessed.